MESSAGE OF THE FATHERS OF THE CHURCH
General Editor: Thomas Halton

Volume 19

MESSAGE OF THE FATHERS OF THE CHURCH

THE EARLY FATHERS ON WAR AND MILITARY SERVICE

by

Louis J. Swift

 Michael Glazier, Inc.
Wilmington, Delaware

ABOUT THE AUTHOR

Louis J. Swift teaches classics at the University of Kentucky and is the Editor of *Patristics*, the newsletter of the North American Patristic Society. He studied at the Gregorian University in Rome and received his doctorate from Johns Hopkins University. He is an expert on social and cultural issues in the patristic era and has written on Ambrose and Augustine as well as the Ante-Nicene writers.

First published in 1983 by Michael Glazier, Inc., 1723 Delaware Avenue, Wilmington, Delaware 19806

Library of Congress Catalog Card Number: 83-81476
International Standard Book Number:
  Message of the Fathers of the Church series:
    (0-89453-312-6, Paper; 0-89453-340-1, Cloth)
  WAR AND MILITARY SERVICE
    (0-89453-330-4, Paper)
    (0-89453-359-2, Cloth)

Cover design by Lillian Brulc

Printed in the United States of America

Uxori carissimae

Contents

Editor's Introduction 11
Acknowledgments 13
Abbreviations 14
Preface 15
Introduction 17

PART I

The Period Before Constantine 32
  1. The Earliest Sources 32
    I Clement, 37.1-4 33
    I Clement, 61.1-2 33
    Justin Martyr, *First Apology,* 39.2-3 34
    Athenagoras, *Plea for Christians,* 37.2-3 35
    Athenagoras, *Plea for Christians,* 1.4 35
    Origin, *Against Celsus,* 8.68 36
  2. Tertullian 38
    Apology, 37.4 38
    Apology, 42.2-3 39
    Apology, 30.4 39
    On Idolatry, 17.2-3 40
    On Idolatry, 19.1-3 41
    On the Crown, 11.1-7 43
    Hippolytus(?), *Apostolic Tradition,* XVI 47
  3. St. Cyprian of Carthage 48
    To Donatus, 6 48
    To Demetrianus, 20 49
  4. Clement of Alexandria 50
    Exhortation, XI.116-117 50
    Exhortation, X.100.2 52

5. Origen...52
   Against Celsus, 8.68.........................53
   Against Celsus, 2.30.........................54
   Against Celsus, 8.73.........................54
   Against Celsus, 3.8..........................56
   Against Celsus, 5.33.........................57
   Against Celsus, 7.26.........................57
   Homilies on Joshua, XV......................59
6. Arnobius 60
7. Lactantius 61
   Divine Institutes, 6.20.9-12 62
   Divine Institutes, 6.20.15-17 62
   Divine Institutes, 6.6.22-24 63
   Divine Institutes, 1.18.8-10 64
   Epitome, 56.3-4.............................65
   On the Death of the Persecutors, 46.1-7........66
   On the Death of the Persecutors, 52.4 67
   Divine Institutes, 1.1.13-16 67
8. Christian Practices 68
   Lactantius, *On the Death of the Persecutors*,
   10.1-4 70
9. The Military Martyrs.........................71
   Acts of Maximilian, 1-2 72
   Acts of Marcellus, 2.1 75
   The Martyrdom of Julius the Veteran, 1.4-3.5 ...76

PART II
The Post-Constantinian Era 80
1. Eusebius of Caesarea 82
   Demonstration of the Gospel, 3.7.140...........83
   In Praise of Constantine, 16.3-7...............84
   In Praise of Constantine, 2.3 85
   Ecclesiastical History, 9.9.5-8 86
   Life of Constantine, 1.6......................87
   Demonstration of the Gospel, 1.8 88
2. Official Church Documents and
   the Eastern Fathers 90

Life of Constantine, 2.33....................90
Council of Nicea, Canon 12 92
Council of Nicea, Canon 14 93
St. Basil of Caesarea, *Epistle* 188.13 94
St. Basil of Caesarea, *Epistle* 106 94
St. Athanasius, *Epistle to Amun* 95
3. St. Ambrose of Milan 96
On the Duties of the Clergy, 3.3.23............98
On Tobias, 15.51...........................99
Discourse on Luke's Gospel, 5.73 100
On the Duties of the Clergy, 3.4.27...........101
On the Duties of the Clergy, 1.36.178.........101
Discourse on Psalm 118, 15.22...............103
Discourse on Psalm 45, 21 104
On the Faith, 2.16.136-43 105
Letter, 25.3 108
On Widows, 8.49 108
Discourse on Luke, 5.58 109
On Jacob, 2.6.29.........................110
4. St. Augustine of Hippo 110
Letter, 153.6.16..........................112
City of God, 15.4 113
City of God, 19.12 114
Letter, 189.6 114
Letter, 229.2 115
City of God, 19.7 116
City of God, 4.15 116
City of God, 19.6 117
City of God, 3.14 118
City of God, 19.7 118
City of God, 17.13 119
Against Faustus, 22.74.....................120
Letter, 138.2.14 122
Against Faustus, 22.79.....................123
On Lord's Sermon, 1.20.63-64 124
Letter, 138.13 126
Letter, 189.4 126
Against Faustus, 22.74.....................127
City of God, 1.21 128

Against Faustus, 22.75 129
City of God, 1.26 130
Letter, 47.5 130
On Free Will, 1.5.11.32-13.41 131
Questions on the Heptateuch, 4.44 135
City of God, 22.6 136
Letter, 229.2 137
Questions on the Heptateuch, 6.10 138
Against Faustus, 22.75 139
Commentary on Psalm 124, 7 140
Letter, 23.7 142
Letter, 34.1 142
Against the Letters of Petilianus, 2.84.186 143
Against the Letters of Petilianus, 2.94.217 144
Letter, 93.3.9 146
Letter, 93.2.8 146
Letter, 93.2.6 147
Commentary on the First Letter of John, 10.7 . . 148
5. Pacifism in the Fourth Century 149
Sulpicius Severus, *Life of St. Martin*, 4 151
Paulinus of Nola, *Letter*, 25.3 152
Prudentius, *Crowns of Martyrdom I*, 34 156

Conclusion 158
For Further Reading 161

EDITOR'S INTRODUCTION

The *Message of the Fathers of the Church* is a companion series to The *Old Testament Message* and The *New Testament Message*. It was conceived and planned in the belief that Scripture and Tradition worked hand in hand in the formation of the thought, life and worship of the primitive Church. Such a series, it was felt, would be a most effective way of opening up what has become virtually a closed book to present-day readers, and might serve to stimulate a revival in interest in Patristic studies in step with the recent, gratifying resurgence in Scriptural studies.

The term "Fathers" is usually reserved for Christian writers marked by orthodoxy of doctrine, holiness of life, ecclesiastical approval and antiquity. "Antiquity" is generally understood to include writers down to Gregory the Great (+604) or Isidore of Seville (+636) in the West, and John Damascene (+749) in the East. In the present series, however, greater elasticity has been encouraged, and quotations from writers not noted for orthodoxy will sometimes be included in order to illustrate the evolution of the Message on particular doctrinal matters. Likewise, writers later than the mid-eighth century will sometimes be used to illustrate the continuity of tradition on matters like sacramental theology or liturgical practice.

An earnest attempt was made to select collaborators on a broad inter-disciplinary and inter-confessional basis, the chief consideration being to match scholars who could handle the Fathers in their original languages with subjects in which they had already demonstrated a special interest and competence. About the only editorial directive given to the selected contributors was that the Fathers, for the most part, should be allowed to speak for themselves and that they should speak in readable, reliable modern English. Volumes on individual themes were considered more suitable than volumes devoted to individual Fathers, each theme, hopefully, contributing an important segment to the total mosaic of the Early Church, one, holy, catholic and apostolic. Each volume has an introductory essay outlining the historical and theological development of the theme, with the body of the work mainly occupied with liberal citations from the Fathers in modern English translation and a minimum of linking commentary. Short lists of Suggested Further Readings are included; but dense, scholarly footnotes were actively discouraged on the pragmatic grounds that such scholarly shorthand has other outlets and tends to lose all but the most relentlessly esoteric reader in a semi-popular series.

At the outset of his *Against Heresies* Irenaeus of Lyons warns his readers "not to expect from me any display of rhetoric, which I have never learned, or any excellence of composition, which I have never practised, or any beauty or persuasiveness of style, to which I make no pretensions." Similarly, modest disclaimers can be found in many of the Greek and Latin Fathers and all too often, unfortunately, they have been taken at their word by an uninterested world. In fact, however, they were often highly educated products of the best rhetorical schools of their day in the Roman Empire, and what they have to say is often as much a lesson in literary and cultural, as well as in spiritual, edification.

St. Augustine, in *The City of God* (19.7), has interesting reflections on the need for a common language in an expanding world community; without a common language a man is more at home with his dog than with a foreigner as far as intercommunication goes, even in the Roman Empire, which imposes on the nations it conquers the yoke of both law and language with a resultant abundance of interpreters. It is hoped that in the present world of continuing language barriers the contributors to this series will prove opportune interpreters of the perennial Christian message.

ACKNOWLEDGMENTS

I would like to thank the University of Kentucky Research Foundation for its support in doing research for this volume and in typing the manuscript. I am also indebted to the University's Inter-Library Loan Service under the direction of Mrs. Vivian Macquown and to the library staff of Lexington Theological Seminary under the direction of Mr. Roscoe M. Pierson. Finally, my thanks to Mrs. Sharon Gill, whose patience and expertise were indispensable in preparing the various drafts, and to the general editor of this series, Professor Thomas Halton for his encouragement and generous assistance.

List of Abbreviations

CCL   *Corpus Christianorum, Series Latina*
CSEL *Corpus Scriptorum Ecclesiasticorum Latinorum*
GCS   *Die griechischen christlichen Schriftsteller der ersten drei Jahrhunderte*
OECT *Oxford Early Christian Texts*
PG   *Patrologia Graeca*
PL   *Patrologia Latina*
TU   *Texte und Untersuchungen*
SC   *Sources Chrétiennes*

PREFACE

In a world of sophisticated weapons and global strategies, of foreign intervention and the pursuit of national self-interest one is justified in questioning whether the Fathers of the Church have anything relevant to say to modern man on war and military service. When military preparedness revolves around missiles and multiple warheads, and when the planning for defense includes preemptory strikes and massive retaliation, it is hard to avoid the suspicion that in the area of war and peace Christian writers of the first four centuries are sadly out of date. In practical terms that suspicion is not unfounded. For pacifists, of course, early Christian arguments against war are as relevant today as they ever were, but for those who take another view it is fair to say that the very notion of the modern state, the intricate character of contemporary international relations and the unending "progress" in the development of armaments all but preclude our finding in these sources any "solution" to the conflict between Christian love and the practice of war.

However, there is more to the sources than that simple fact. The problem which war and military service posed for Christians in the early Church, albeit in a context much simpler than our own, was real, and the specific issues that they wrestled with have not gone out of style. We can profit, for example, from seeing how they tried to reconcile Old Testament wars with the peaceful import of the Gospels. We can learn from their efforts to live up to the Sermon on the Mount both when they had little involvement in the affairs of state and when they were deeply immersed in the exercise of power. We can gain insight from watching as they defend the Christians' loyalty to Rome and then spell out the meaning of that term in times of peace and war. Knowing how issues like these were handled in the early Church and how each response was circumscribed by place and time cannot help but clarify a problem which no age has brought to resolution. For that we should be grateful and in some sense satisfied.

INTRODUCTION

In light of the attention given in the New Testament to the virtues of love, patience and forgiveness, one would be hard pressed to find a human activity that is seemingly more at odds with the spirit of the Gospels than violence and war. If the God of the Old Testament permitted and sometimes enjoined his people to take up the sword, the God of the New warns us about the fate of those who follow that path, and his own message is rightfully described as a "Gospel of Peace" (*Ephes.* 6.15). From the angels' greeting at Bethlehem (*Luke* 2.14), through Jesus' admonition to Peter about putting away the sword (*Mt.* 26.52) to the risen Christ's greeting in the upper room (*Luke* 24.36; *John* 20.19), the pervasive spirit of the new dispensation is consistently non-violent. Jesus' injunction about "turning the other cheek" (*Mt.* 5.38-39) is the clearest but not the only statement about the ideal to be pursued where violence is concerned, and his own life and death underscored the pacific character of the Christian faith. If violence has any place in the Christian's life, it would appear that it must be a violence which is endured rather than inflicted, a violence which is suffered in imitation of the Founder as a way of transcending human passions and breaking the endless cycle of injury and retaliation.

Following this train of thought one would expect to find in early Christian literature a fairly straightforward presentation and elaboration of pacifist ideas, and that is largely what we get from writers of the first three centuries who deal with the issues of war, violence and military service in any detail. Not surprisingly Christ's remarks in the Sermon on the Mount are frequently cited in support of non-violence (e.g. Justin Martyr, *First Apology* 16.1-4; Athenagoras, *Plea on Behalf of the Christians* 1.4; Tertullian, *On Patience* 8.2; Origen, *Against Celsus* 7.25), and it is not uncommon for Christians to be described as living in the age of peace foretold by Isaiah (2.3-4) and Micah (4.2-3). Writing in the second century, Justin Martyr says to his Jewish opponent Tryphon, "We who were filled with war, mutual slaughter, and every other form of evil have everywhere transformed our instruments of war, fashioning our swords into ploughshares and our spears into farm tools. We are now cultivators of piety, justice, generosity, faith and the hope which comes from the Father through him who was crucified" (*Dialogue with Tryphon* 110.3). In his own way Irenaeus picks up the same theme in his treatise *Against Heresies* (4.34.4), and Tertullian uses the passage from Isaiah as a way of distinguishing the New Law from the Old: "For the practice of the Old Law was to avenge itself with the sword, to take an eye for an eye and to repay injury for injury. But the practice of the New Law was to focus on clemency and to turn bloodthirsty swords and lances to peaceful uses and to change the warlike acts against rivals and enemies into the peaceful pursuits of plowing and farming the land" (*Against the Jews* 3.10). Origen, too, appeals to this passage of Isaiah when he tries to explain where the Christians originated: "We have come in response to Jesus' commands to beat into plowshares the rational swords of conflict and arrogance and to change into pruning hooks those spears that we used to fight with. For we no longer take up the sword against any nation, nor do we learn the art of war any more...We have become sons of peace through Jesus our leader..." (*Against Celsus* 5.33).

Nonetheless, from the very outset there were problems in reducing early Christian teachings on this issue to a single point of view. Not only does the New Testament contain texts that are ambiguous or positively ill-suited to a pacifist outlook, but more than one of these passages could be interpreted in a quite opposite sense. If Christ extolled the peacemakers, he also had high praise for the centurion at Capernaum (*Mt.* 8.5-13). If he pointedly refused to use force for his own protection during the Passion (*John* 18. 36), he also talked about rendering to Caesar what was Caesar's (*Mt.* 22.21), and he did not turn the other cheek when the servant of the High Priest struck him (*John* 18.23). Moreover, if the military profession were intrinsically incompatible with the Christian faith, it would be difficult to explain why John the Baptist said nothing about abandoning the service to the soldiers who came to him for advice (*Luke* 3.14), or why Peter had no reservations about baptizing the centurion Cornelius (*Acts* 10), or why Paul was silent about the official responsibilities of the gaoler whom he converted at Philippi (*Acts* 16.27-34).

The problem is compounded, of course, by the vivid descriptions of the Lord's final coming which we read in the *Book of Revelation.* Not only is the end of all things to be marked by wars, but Christ himself is portrayed as a victorious general (*Rev.* 3.21; 5.5; 6.2) from whose mouth springs a two-edged sword (1.16; 2.12; 19.15). As a "warrior for justice" he leads "the armies of heaven" and will conquer the beast and the kings of the earth (19.11-21). His own reign will be followed by wars against Gog and Magog and will eventually result in the victory of the saints (20.7-10). If it is true that these figurative descriptions cannot be taken as an endorsement of any ethical position on war or violence, it is also true that they formed part of the very substance of Christian thought. They gave concrete shape to Christian expectations of triumph, and if the vision of the Christian community as an army at war with the beast of temporal power is neither a constant nor a dominant image in early Christian literature, it is something to be reckoned with in arguing a pacifist position.

Wars of the Old Testament, on the other hand, were obviously not figurative, and these, too, compounded the problem of non-violence in the early Church. Except for the gnostics, like Marcion, who rejected the Old Testament as a source of revelation, Christians had to deal with the fact that Yahweh not only sanctioned wars but assisted the Israelites against their enemies. Thus, we find Moses extolling the victory over Pharaoh and praising Yahweh the warrior whose right hand "shatters the enemy" (*Exodus* 15.1-18; cf. *Numbers* 10.35); we see Gideon being instructed in how to proceed against the Midianites (*Judges* 7.2-25), and we read of Joshua's being told by God to use strategy against the king of Ai (*Joshua* 8). In this connection it is hard to overlook the harshness with which Israel treated its foes (*Deuteronomy* 20.15-18) and the fury which the Levites unleashed against those Jews who worshiped the Golden Calf (*Exodus* 32.25-29). The difficulty posed by these examples was expressed very succinctly long ago by Adolf von Harnack, "How can man issue a general condemnation of wars if God himself called for them and directed them?" Indeed, Christian pride in Israelite victories won with God's assistance is evident as early as Stephen and Paul (*Acts* 7.45; 13.17-20), and the author of *Hebrews* does not hesitate to extol the faith of Old Testament figures who wielded the sword: "There is not time for me to give an account of Gideon, Barak, Samson, Jephthah, or of David, Samuel and the prophets. These were men who through faith conquered kingdoms, did what is right and earned the promises. They could keep a lion's mouth shut, put out blazing fires and emerge unscathed from battle. They were weak people who were given strength, to be brave in war and drive back foreign invaders" (11.32-34).

The tendency to include Old Testament warriors in the list of Christian models is not surprising, as we shall see, for writers like Ambrose and Augustine who believed that Israel's wars were clear evidence that at least some forms of coercion were legitimate. What is remarkable is that even those authors who speak mostly in pacifist terms take a rather positive stance toward Old Testament wars. Thus Justin Martyr claims that the Israelites took possession of Canaan "according to God's will" (*Dialogue with Tryphon* 139) and that God himelf slew the Assyrians in the time of Ezechia (*ibid.* 83). In a similar vein he describes Joshua as a type of Christ, and he sees Moses' outstretched arms in the battle against Amalek as a figure of the cross (*ibid.* 91). Allegorical interpretations like these latter in which the full meaning of the text is discernible only in Christian terms are common to writers of the period (cf. Irenaeus, *Against Heresies* 4.24; Tertullian, *Against Marcion* 3.18.6) and are sometimes used as a way of explaining —or explaining away—Old Testament wars (see, for example, Origen, *Homilies on Joshua* 15.1). But however much this point might be argued or however much Tertullian will insist that Christ's message of peace has superseded the ethics of the Old Law, it was difficult, as he discovered, to extol the warriors of Israel on the one hand and to argue a pacifist position on the other.

The difficulty is increased by the fact that military metaphors abound in the New Testament descriptions of the Christian life. Paul's writings and the pastoral epistles are a case in point. In addition to the well-known passage from I Thessalonians (5.8) where the Apostle talks about the breastplate of faith and love and the helmet of salvation, he reminds the Ephesians to put on God's armor because they are struggling not against human enemies but against "Sovereignties and Powers who originate the darkness in this world, the spiritual army of evil in the heavens" (*Ephesians* 6.12). Elsewhere (II *Corinthians* 6.7) the faithful are described as "being armed with the weapons of righteousness;" Paul's assistants are addressed as fellow soldiers (*Philippians* 2.25; *Philemon* 2), and his friend Timothy is advised to bear up under difficulties "like a good soldier of Christ Jesus" (II *Timothy* 2.3).

In none of these texts or others like them can it be argued that the author was endorsing the notion of Christian participation in war. Indeed, in two passages (II *Cor.* 10.3-6; *Ephes.* 6.12) Paul explicitly states that he is talking about war only in a spiritual sense. But the long-range impact of this imagery must not be dismissed entirely. If a modern commentator argues that military metaphors in Paul and later Christian writers "no more *prove* (italics added) that the Church encouraged or even approved of war than the less frequent allusions to the games and the theatre prove that these were sanctioned by the conscience of the primitive Christians" (Moffat, 657), that truth is not the whole truth. The fact that somehow the concept of a "sacred warfare" (*sacra militia*) could be incorporated into Christianity whereas there was never anything like a "sacred prostitution" or a "sacred homicide" should not be overlooked. If the latter two concepts are totally foreign to the Christian faith, we must ask why the same was not true of military analogies. Somehow there was a noble and praiseworthy dimension to *militia* itself which Christian writers found congenial to their purposes. In a manner akin to the metaphors of athletic contests, this dimension was a separable element that was compatible with Christian faith and that allowed even an avowed pacifist like Tertullian to use military imagery in great profusion. Whatever arguments can be made for distinguishing spiritual and temporal warfare, it is hard to escape the impact of the metaphors themselves. Rational distinctions and disclaimers are not sufficient to dispel the ambiguities generated by such language.

Thus far we have been preoccupied with the Christian community's evaluation of its own religious traditions as they relate to the issue of war and violence. An equally significant aspect of the problem is the Christians' attitude toward temporal power and the role it plays—positive or negative—in the development of the Kingdom of God on earth. In this area the issue of war and violence becomes rather acute because the use of force is at the very heart of government, and pacifist principles appear to undercut the coercive power that a state must have to maintain its own existence against internal or external threats. Without attempting anything like a thorough discussion of Church-State relations in the early Christian centuries, we should consider certain dimensions of this relationship since they have considerable impact on Christian attitudes concerning the legitimacy of violence and war.

Through a selective reading of New Testament texts and early apologetic writings it is possible to view the Christian community as a race set apart from other men, a persecuted minority fighting for survival against a society and a government that was consistently hostile to it. Such a view of Christianity is found in the *Book of Revelation*, where Rome is depicted as a beast that blasphemes God and makes war on the saints (*Revelation* 13) or as a harlot that is drunk with the blood of the "Martyrs of Jesus" (*Revelation* 17). Quite naturally a negative view of temporal power prevails during periods of persecution, and echoes of it can be heard in the apologetic writers of the second and third centuries (see, for example, Hippolytus, *Commentary on Daniel* 4.8.7-8). With a few notable exceptions, however, persecutions tended to be sporadic and short-lived, and it is remarkable how inconstant Christian writers were in their opposition to Rome.

Much of the reason for this latter fact is the conciliatory attitude toward temporal authority that we find in St. Paul and in other Scriptural texts. In *Romans* 13 the Apostle says, quite simply, "You must all obey the governing authorities. Since all government comes from God, the civil authorities were appointed by God, and so anyone who resists authority is rebelling against God's decision...The state is there to serve God for your benefit. If you break the law, however, you may well have fear; the bearing of the sword has its significance. The authorities are there to serve God; they carry out God's revenge by punishing wrongdoers" (1-4). If Paul says nothing here about the legitimacy of government, the rights of rulers or Christian involvement in the exercise of temporal power, he at least views such power as a source of justice, and he reminds the Christians that they are subject no less than other men to those agencies which preserve a form of order. This position was adopted by more than one Christian writer of the first three centuries (e.g. Irenaeus,

Against Heresies 5.24.1-3; Tertullian, *Scorpiace* 14), and, as we shall see, the Apostle's words to the Romans strongly influenced the thinking of both Ambrose and Augustine on war and the use of force.

Even more explicit acceptance of the state's role in maintaining an ordered society is found in I *Timothy* 2.1-2, where the author advises that prayers be offered "for everyone—petitions, intercessions and thanksgiving—and especially for kings and others in authority so that we may be able to live religious and reverent lives in peace and quiet." As we shall see, this advice is followed by early Christian writers to the point where such appeals for the security and peace of the empire become commonplace. I *Peter* 2.13-17 goes a step further in recommending that Christians set a good example and win pagan approval by their responsible behavior: "For the sake of the Lord, accept the authority of every social institution: the emperor as the supreme authority, and the governors as commissioned by him to punish criminals and praise good citizenship. God wants you to be good citizens so as to silence what fools are saying in their ignorance.... Fear God and honor the emperor." Texts like these suggest that intransigent and indiscriminate opposition to temporal power by Christians is misplaced. If it is not infrequently argued that Christians are different from other men, it is also claimed in the words of Tertullian (*Apology* 42.1) that they are not "Brahmins, naked sages from India, forest dwellers or exiles from everyday life," and that they have as much loyalty to the state as their pagan colleagues. As one modern commentator has put it, "The Roman State is *their* State; that which damages the State also damages them; that which is beneficial to the State is beneficial to them also" (Aland, 124).

In fact, from the Christian's point of view, the benefits do not all flow in one direction. Addressing the emperor Marcus Aurelius and his son Commodus toward the end of the second century, Melito, Bishop of Sardis, is recorded to have made the point that Christianity was a boon to the Empire. "Our philosophy [i.e. Christianity] flourished at first among the barbarians, but it reached its full bloom among your people during the great reign of your forebear Augustus, and it became an especially good omen for your realm. From that time on Rome's power increased in size and splendor. You are, and with your son you will continue to be, Augustus' happy successor, provided you protect the philosophy whose origin and growth coincided with his rule. Your ancestors had respect for this philosophy along with other cults and the best proof that the concomitant flourishing of our doctrine and the noble development of the empire was all to the good is the fact that from the time of Augustus' reign the realm has suffered no harm. On the contrary, it has experienced only what is magnificent and glorious in accord with all men's aspirations" (Eusebius, *Ecclesiastical History* 4.26.7-8). A similar vision of the mutually supportive role that God intended for Christianity and the Empire is found elsewhere in Christian writers of the first three centuries (cf. Irenaeus, *Against Heresies* 4.30.3; Tertullian, *On the Pallium* 2; Origen, *Against Celsus* 2.30), and after Constantine's accession this concept heavily influenced Christian thinking about the nature of temporal power.

Where Christians drew the line in paying allegiance to the state was in the area of idolatry (i.e. emperor-worship), but in refusing that kind of homage they did not refuse their loyalty. Writing around 170 A.D. Theophilus, Bishop of Antioch, puts the issue very simply, "I will honor the emperor not by worshipping him, but by offering prayers for him...He is not God. He is a man whom God has appointed to give just judgment, not to be worshipped" (*To Autolycus* 1.11). When the issue of idolatry was resolved at the time of Constantine in the fourth century, the principal source of opposition to the state was removed, and the fundamentally positive outlook which had existed from the beginning began to show itself with less reserve or, as some scholars argue, with undue enthusiasm. That development settled certain issues that had been debated for centuries, but, as will become evident, it created new ones that were equally intractable.

Thus, on the basis of the Christians' own Scriptural traditions concerning war and military service in both the Old and New Testaments, and on the basis of their general view of the role of the state in society, there seems to have been insufficient grounds for a clear-cut Christian consensus on the legitimacy of war and violence. More importantly, perhaps, there appears to have been no pressing reason for coming to grips with the problem at all during the first two centuries after Christ. As a group Christians were not actually responsible for maintaining or directing the institutions of government, and their duties to the state were fulfilled largely by obeying the laws and living peacefully. They had little or no expectation that the Empire would ever become Christian, and writers tended to concentrate on problems more internal to the community. It is not surprising, then, that we find relatively little discussion of broader social issues including the Christian's role in maintaining the peace and security of the Empire.

In practical terms conversion to Christianity during this period seems to have had little impact on the question of military service. References to Christians in the army at this time are limited to the very few already cited from the New Testament, and one has the impression that Paul's advice "Let everyone stay as he was at the time of his call" (I *Corinthians* 7.20) was being taken to heart by soldier-converts no less than by others. At least until the end of the second century we have no evidence of anyone's abandoning the service on religious grounds, and it is safe to assume that the number of military converts at this time was rather small. With respect to entering the army after conversion, the violence and excesses often associated with a military career as well as the idolatry connected with camp life must have discouraged Christians from volunteering. Indeed, it has been argued by some scholars that the opportunities for doing so were quite limited since recruitment in the legions was restricted to Roman citizens, and Christians by and large did not belong to this class. Whatever position one takes on the social status of the early converts, this argument is weakened by the fact that auxiliary troops were commonly drawn from sla es and other non-citizens. What remains true, however, is that involuntary conscription is not attested in the sources before the fourth century, and anyone who had scruples about a military career could easily avoid getting involved. In sum, the whole question of war, violence and military service must have seemed quite irrelevant for Christians in the early Church, and this fact undoubtedly accounts for the paucity of evidence on the issue during this time.

The situation changes dramatically, however, during the course of the third and fourth centuries. In the third we see the development of strong pacifist arguments in the writings of men like Tertullian and Origen, and in the fourth century advocates of the just war such as Ambrose and Augustine take a quite opposite stance. In the developments that took place during these years it is clear that the reign of Constantine (312-337 A.D.) represents a turning point in Christian thinking about the legitimacy of violence and war. By and large writers before him tended to be pacifist in outlook, whereas those following his rise to power argued for the legitimacy of war under certain conditions. It is a mistake, however, to note only the discontinuities that are apparent in this change of outlook. When the two periods (pre-Constantinian and post-Constantinian) are characterized as pacifist and non-pacifist, each full-blown in its own way, a false dichotomy is established, and the new attitude toward Christian participation in war that grew up in the fourth century appears as a kind of *volteface*. We are then tempted to see this change as abandonment of principles and the adoption of a policy of expediency after the interests of Church and state had become synonomous.

That kind of assessment is overly simplified. If it is presumptuous to say that there were two traditions in the period before Constantine, it is at least clear that there were two sides to the issue. The most vocal and the most articulate side was pacifist. In this school Tertullian, Origen and the early Lactantius stand out as the most reflective and persuasive writers. Although they do not all agree on the reasons for opposing Christian participation in war or military service, although they are not of one mind on the amount of cooperation they will allow a Christian in such matters, and although they are not always consistent in their own thinking on the subject, they leave no doubt that for them violence of any kind is incompatible with the demands of the Christian faith.

The other side is non-pacifist. It has no apologists that we know of, and no articulated rationale. Both the fact of its existence and the arguments on which it is based are gleaned indirectly from a very few sources. When, for example, Tertullian in his treatise *On the Crown* commends a Christian soldier for renouncing the service, he notes that this individual represented an exception to the rule. If the legionnaire's colleagues did not share his problem of conscience about military service, we cannot assume that they had abandoned the practice of the faith or that they were grossly insensitive to Christian principles concerning love of neighbor. They simply disagreed with him on the issue. Elsewhere (*On Idolatry* 19) Tertullian says that no Christian could stay in the army despite the fact that the Jews fought wars, the centurion at Capernaum believed in Christ and the soldiers consulted John the Baptist about their obligations in life. It appears, then, that these examples from Scripture were being cited by some as reasons for not following a strictly pacifist line of thought, and the very fact that Tertullian speaks at length about the moral dimensions of military service is evidence that the whole issue had not been settled in the Christian community. Later, at the end of the third century, this fact becomes even more evident when we learn that the emperors' bodyguard itself included Christian troops and that Diocletian began his persecution by seeking out Christians in the army.

What all this means is that, concomitant with the strong statements of Christian writers about the inherent contradiction between military service and Christian principles of love, a significant number of the faithful were somehow finding it possible to reconcile the two things in their own minds. How this was done we are at a loss to explain in any detail although it is clear that, as time moved on, military duty for some members of the army was little more than a civic function. What is significant, however, is that opposing views on this issue developed side by side during the early centuries and that neither of them was strong enough to displace the other. Thus, we are hardly justified in talking about a simple reversal in Christian thinking about these matters in the period after Constantine when the Church achieved a privileged status in the Empire. Indeed there was no indiscriminate endorsement by the post-Constantinian Church of the Empire's efforts to maintain peace within and outside its borders. If Christians in the fourth century acknowledged the legitimacy of war and military service, they also found it necessary to circumscribe the rights of the state to employ coercion. In neither period, then, are we dealing with absolutes. The change that occurred represents a major shift rather than a reversal in Christian thinking, a shift that was made possible by earlier ambiguities and disagreements concerning the use of coercion and made necessary by the altered political circumstances in which Christians now found themselves.

In this volume my purpose will be to allow the works of the Fathers themselves to reveal the various developments which took place in Christian thinking about war, violence and military service during the first four centuries A.D. On this issue our information is scattered and sometimes very indirect because we have no such thing as a treatise on the morality of war. Even a writer like Augustine, who had more to say on the subject than anyone else, never dealt with the problem in a separate discourse. Thus, we are forced to glean the relevant material from comments made in a variety of contexts. I have attempted to set forth the principal texts on the issue, to clarify the various positions which early Christian writers adopted and to explain their reasons for doing so. This latter is very important because it helps us to see why developments on the issue took the direction they did. On more than one occasion what appeared to a particular author as an unalterable assump-

tion about society and politics turned out not to be so, and
when new conditions arose, new solutions were called for.
By assuming, for example, that the Roman emperor would
always be pagan, Tertullian never even considered the
question of what should be done if a Christian became
commander-in-chief of the army. When the impossible did
occur in the fourth century, the whole issue of war and
military service assumed a dimension that Tertullian did
not envision. Again, when Origen claimed that a pagan
emperor could wage a just war but that Christians could
participate only through prayer, he assumed a kind of
dichotomy in the community that simply did not obtain in
the fourth century. Accordingly, when violent threats to
the empire arose, a Christian emperor with Christian subjects had to find solutions that were more nuanced than
Origen ever thought possible.

     To some degree, at least, the changes which took place in
the fourth century reflect a change in self-perception on the
part of the Church, i.e. away from a sectarian self-image in
the direction of an ecclesial one. The classic distinction
made by Ernst Troeltsch seventy years ago between two
socio-religious types of organizations (viz. the "sect-type"
and the "church-type") is a convenient method of concep-
tualizing, although not explaining, the relative abandonment of pacifist principles in the period after Constantine.
According to the sectarian construct the religious community is seen as a small select group centered often
enough around a charismatic leader and given to a form of
perfectionism. It directs almost all its attention to sanctify-
ing its own members according to some idealistic and absolute principles of orthodoxy and takes little cognizance of
what others think. It seeks not so much to be a leaven in
the larger community as to be a model which stands apart
and invites others to come in. Whether its adherents are
hostile, tolerant or indifferent to the world outside, they
generally refuse to have anything to do with oaths or
courts of law and they serve neither as magistrates nor as
combatants in the armed services.

In the ecclesial or "church-type" construct, on the other hand, the community of believers is viewed as a hierarchial structure with a basically conservative social outlook. It "seeks to exert a spiritual influence upon the whole of life through becoming an integral part of existing society," and to accomplish this aim, "it compromises by adapting the absolute law of God to the relativities and exigencies of living in an imperfect world" (Marrin, 4-5). In this vision of things full cognizance is taken of human sin whose existence makes it impossible for most men to live up fully to the requirements of the Gospel as long as the world continues to be what it is. In this context the ideal is a goal to be pursued but one that is realized only in another world, and the task of the Church is to make that goal as accessible to all men as the limits of its own integrity will permit.

These two models of the Church are neither the only nor, perhaps, the most illuminating constructs for revealing the essential nature of the Christian community. They are, after all, abstract configurations intended as an aid in understanding two kinds of thinking about Christian obligations vis-a-vis the larger community. With respect to the issue of war, violence and military service, however, they are illuminating because, during the first three centuries, Christian thinking in this area reflects the mentality of the "sect-type" whereas after that time it is closer to the outlook of the "church-type." It will be beneficial, then, as we examine the texts from both periods to keep this distinction in mind, being aware all the while that both constructs are detectable in each period, sometimes within the thinking of a single author.

PART I

THE PERIOD BEFORE CONSTANTINE

1. The Earliest Sources

As already noted, the theoretical nature of the problem of war and military service for Christians in the first two centuries afforded little occasion for protracted discussion of the issue. Thus, our information about what Christians actually thought about the matter must be derived from general comments and indirect references. Such sources will provide a feel for some of the ambiguities involved, but they give us nothing like the articulated positions which come later with Tertullian and Origen. Our earliest non-scriptural evidence is found in the *First Letter of Clement*, a pastoral epistle written to the Christian community at Corinth around the end of the first century A.D. urging a quick settlement of internal strife. In appealing for unity and harmony the author, who is traditionally identified as the third successor of Peter in Rome, cites the model of military leadership in the Roman army and in doing so he seems to go beyond the mere use of metaphor.

37.1-4[1] With all zeal, then, Brethren, let us serve as good
soldiers under his [i.e. Christ's] irreproachable
command. Let us remember the discipline, obedience and submission that our government troops
exhibit when they carry out orders. It is not everyone's job to lead a thousand men, or a hundred,
or fifty or some such number. Each one carries out
the orders of the emperor and the governors
according to his own rank. Those with great
responsibility cannot do without those who have
less and vice-versa. Together they form a kind of
whole, and therein lies the benefit (37.1-4).

Whether the hierarchical concept of service that is extolled
here springs from Stoicism or from the biblical idea of the
people of God in the desert, it is clear that the military
model is considered a proper one for Christian action. If
the text does not endorse Christian participation in war,
one would nonetheless have difficulty in reconciling it with
a pacifist stance. The fact that the author is not at all
embarrassed by such imagery very likely indicates that the
problem of Christians' serving in the army was not an issue
for him. At the same time, however, toward the end of the
letter he has no reservations about expressing a genuine
loyalty to the Empire and a hope that earthly rulers will
exercise their God-given power responsibly.

61.1-2[2] Through your own magnificent and indescribable
power you yourself, O Master, have granted them
[i.e. earthly rulers and leaders] their royal authority. You did so in order that we might recognize the
glory and honor you have conferred upon them
and thus follow your will in being submissive to
them. Grant them, O Lord, health, peace, harmony
and stability in order that they may exercise this
sovereign power which they have received from
you without giving offense. It is you, Heavenly

[1]Text: SC 167.160.
[2]Text: SC 167.198.

> Master, Ruler of the Ages, who give to the sons of
> men glory, honor and power over earthly things.
> Guide their decisions yourself, O Lord, according
> to what is good and acceptable in your eyes so that
> by dutifully wielding in peace and gentleness the
> authority you gave them they may gain your favor.
> (61.1-2).[2]

Prayers of this kind, which echo the Pauline admonitions
of *Romans*, chap. 13, and the Pastoral epistles, become common in the second century, and the fact that they appear
even among those writers who take it for granted that
bloodshed has no place in the Christian community is an
indication that as yet the issue of war and military service
was neither pressing nor well articulated.

Writing about 150 A.D. Justin Martyr claims that Christians pay their taxes, obey the authorities, and pray that
the emperor be blessed with "sound judgment," but he also
assumes that the faithful are living in a new age which
eschews violence in all its forms. Although formerly they
killed one another, Christians now pray for their enemies
(*First Apology* 14) and follow the injunction of Christ
about turning the other cheek (16). They are living in the
time which was prophesied by Isaiah and which demands a
new ethic.

> 39.2-3[3] When the Prophetic Spirit speaks and foretells the
> future, he says, 'The Law shall come out of Sion
> and the Lord's word from Jerusalem. And he will
> judge the Gentiles and reproach many people, and
> they will beat their swords into plows and their
> spears into pruning hooks. And nation will not
> raise its sword against nation, and they will no
> longer learn the arts of war.' You can believe that
> this prophecy, too, was fulfilled. For twelve men,
> ignorant and unskilled in speaking as they were,
> went out from Jerusalem to the world, and with the
> help of God announced to every race of men that they

---

[3]Text: PG 6.388.

had been sent by Christ to teach the word of God to everyone, and we who formerly killed one another not only refuse to make war on our enemies but in order to avoid lying to our interrogators or deceiving them, we freely go to our deaths confessing Christ (*First Apology* 39.2-3)

The same sentiments of loyalty and the same insistence that Christians abstain from bloodshed are to be found about twenty-five years later in Athenagoras' *Plea for the Christians*, which is, as it were, an open letter addressed to the emperor, Marcus Aurelius, and his son, Commodus. Written around 177 A.D. the work echoes the words of I *Timothy* 2.2 in arguing that Christians are just as much interested in a peaceful world as their pagan colleagues are.

37.2-3[4] Who are more justified in receiving what they ask for than people like ourselves? We pray for your reign in order that the succession may pass from father to son, as is most fitting, and that your sway may increase and expand as everyone becomes subject to you. Such a development benefits us, too, inasmuch as we can both lead a life of quiet and peace, and do willingly everything that is enjoined upon us (37.2-3).

At the same time the author expresses confusion over the charges of murder and cannibalism that are leveled at the Christians since they refuse even to see legally condemned men put to death in the gladiatorial shows. "Watching a man being slain is next to killing him," Athenagoras says (35.5), and Christians must follow Christ's injunction in the Sermon on the Mount.

1.4[5] We have learned not to return blow for blow or to take to court those who rob or plunder us. What is more, if they strike us abusively on one side of the

---

[4]Text: OECT, ed. Schoedel, 86.
[5]Text: OECT, 4.

head, we have learned to offer the other as well and to give our cloak to anyone who takes our tunic (1.4).

The bloodshed discussed in these passages and elsewhere in the Greek apologists is largely associated with gladiatorial combats, judicial processes (which included torture and sometimes execution in the arena) or cases of murder. The authors are preoccupied with stressing the peaceful character of Christianity, and issues such as the legitimacy of war itself or Christian participation in it do not come up. Though Justin's pupil Tatian may claim that wars are inspired by demons (*Address to the Greeks* 19.2-4) and may himself refuse a military command (*ibid* 11.1), and though Athenagoras (*On the Resurrection* 19.7) may take it for granted that those who slay countless thousands in their efforts to gain power or wealth will not go unpunished, such statements tell us little about specific problems created by war and military service. Quite probably because Christians did not find themselves in the army to any great extent, the necessity for facing the issue was not much more urgent than it had been in St. Paul's day. Loyalty to the state had little or nothing to do with military service; hence the one could be affirmed without coming to grips in any way with the other.

However, precisely when Athenagoras was writing, we begin to get indications that the situation was changing. In the years between 177-180 A.D. the pagan writer Celsus, a knowledgeable and sophisticated critic of the new religion, mounted an attack on Christianity in a treatise which is entitled *The True Discourse* and which is known to us from Origen's reply, *Against Celsus*, written some seventy years later. In his work Celsus argued that the Christians' refusal to pay divine honor to the Emperor had some very practical effects:

8.68[6]   "If everyone followed your example, nothing would prevent his [i.e. the emperor's] being left all

[6]Text: SC 150,330

alone and deserted while all earthly affairs fell under the sway of the most lawless and uncivilized barbarians, and no one on earth heard anything about your religion or the true wisdom" (*Against Celsus* 8.68).

These words indicate that for at least one pagan writer the Christians' unwillingness to honor the emperor in traditional ways had some threatening implications. Emperor-worship and defense of the realm went hand in hand; one could not refuse the one without endangering the other. We will see more on this problem when we examine Origen's views below, but it is fair to say that by the end of the second century the whole question of whether Christian attitudes toward violence and war could be reconciled with the necessities of state was at least being raised in some quarters.

At the same time, however, there is evidence to suggest that Celsus was not wholly informed when he claimed that Christians refused to do their part to protect the Empire. For it was during the reign of Marcus Aurelius (161-180 A.D.) that the legend of the Twelfth Legion (*Legio XII fulminata*) and the Miracle of the Rain arose. According to the accounts of this event given by Tertullian (*Apology* 5.6; *To Scapula* 4.6) and Eusebius (*Ecclesiastical History* 5.5.1-6) the Roman legion in its campaign against the Germans and Sarmatians was hard pressed at one point by thirst and was on the verge of a serious defeat. Through the prayer of Christian troops on the battleline a saving rain occurred, which brought relief to the Roman army and enabled it eventually to triumph. Although the Christians' role in this event is called into question by the fact that pagan sources recount the story without mentioning them (Dio Cassius 72.14.8; *Lives of the Later Caesars, Marcus Antoninus,* 24.4), the historicity of that detail is not the point here. What is significant is that there was a sufficient number of Christians in the Twelfth Legion to gain credence for the account in the Christian community and that their presence in the army created no apparent scandal. It seems safe to assume that Christian soldiers were in the legion for some time prior to 173 A.D., the approximate date of the event, and that fact would be easy to explain because Melitene, the city in Cappadocia in which the legion was stationed, had a considerable number of Christians.

2. *Tertullian (c. 160 — c. 220 A.D.)*

It is ironic in some ways that Tertullian should cite this instance of Christian activity in the army as an example of loyalty to Rome. For he is the first Church writer to wrestle with the issue of military service in a concrete way, and his attitude toward Christian participation in war is anything but sympathetic. It is fair to say that he is the first articulate spokesman for pacifism in the Christian Church. In considering his views, however, we must remember that he was a very polemical writer, who perhaps more than any other apologist of the pre-Constantinian era tended to tailor his argument to the issue of the moment. If he takes a rather trenchant position against Christian participation in war, he is not always consistent on this point. Thus, in his *Apology*, which was written around 197 A.D. and which is a plea for fair treatment of the Christians, a certain amount of ambiguity is created by the pride he takes in the spread of Christianity even to the camps.

> 37.4[7] We started yesterday and already we have filled the world and everything that belongs to you—the cities, apartment houses, fortresses, towns, market places, the camps themselves, your tribes, town councils, the imperial palace, the Senate, the Forum. The only thing we have left to you are the temples. We can count your armies; there is a greater number of Christians in one province! What kind of war would we, who willingly submit to the sword, not be ready or eager for despite our

[7]Text: CCL 1.148.

inferior numbers if it were not for the fact that according to our doctrine it is more permissible to be killed than to kill (37.4).

If there is obvious exaggeration here about the strength of the Christians in the Empire, there is little reason to doubt the fact that they permeated society. In fact, later in the same work Tertullian reiterates this point:

> 42.2-3[8]Thus, we live in the world sharing with you the forum, the market, the baths, the shops, the factories, the inns, the market days and all other commercial activities. We, no less than you, sail the sea, serve in the army, farm the land, buy and sell (42.2-3).

At the same time he underscores both the loyalty of the Christians to the Empire and their reasons for desiring its continued well-being:

> 30.4[9] We pray without ceasing for all emperors, for their prolonged life, for a secure empire, for protection of the imperial palace, for brave armies, a loyal Senate, an upright citizenry, a peaceful world and for everything that the emperor desires as a man and as a Caesar (30.4). . . . There is another, more pressing obligation on us to pray for the emperors, for the whole world, for Rome's imperial government and its affairs. We know that Rome's continuance holds back the great force which menaces the world, that is, the very end of time which threatens frightful calamities. We have no desire to experience these things, and while we pray for their deferral, we are promoting the continued existence of Rome (30.4).

Thus, there is a kind of tension in Tertullian's thought over the issue of Christian participation in war and military service. If, as we shall see, he takes a strong stand

[8]Text: CCL 1.157.
[9]Text: CCL 1.141-142.

against it, the reason is not that he can make no distinction between murder and killing in war (cf. *On the Resurrection* 16.7-8), that he was fundamentally opposed to Rome or that he hoped for the swift arrival of the Parousia. In fact, quite the opposite is true (cf. *On the Resurrection* 24.18). He had no taste for Armageddon and was a realist about the need for securing the Empire's borders. At the same time, however, he recognized the growing presence of Christians in the army, and the problem this posed for him was quite simple: he could not reconcile that fact with the Scriptures.

His first attempt to deal with the issue in detail comes in the treatise *On Idolatry*, a work which is usually dated some fourteen years after the *Apology* but which may very well be contemporary with it. As the title of the treatise indicates, its theme is the danger that paganism posed to the Christian community at all levels of social and political activity. Among the issues raised in this connection was the question of whether or not a Christian could hold public office in the state or could serve in the army without compromising his faith. Tertullian's sardonic reply to the first point leaves little doubt about his scepticism on the matter.

17.2-3[10]   A dispute has arisen of late whether a servant of God can hold a position of honor or authority as long as he can stay free of any appearance of idolatry by means of some special grace or his own cleverness after the manner of Joseph and Daniel. These men functioned as governors of all Egypt or Babylonia, enjoying the honor, power and trappings of office but remaining free of idolatry. We may grant that somebody could hold a position in a purely honorary way if you can believe that it is possible for him to avoid sacrificing or authorizing sacrifices, paying for victims, managing the upkeep of temples, taking care of temple taxes, putting on shows at his own or at public expense, or presiding

[10]Text: CCL 2.1118.

over the staging of shows, issuing solemn pronunci-
ations or edicts or even taking an oath. Provided he
can do this and also avoid the functions of his
office, i.e. making judicial decisions affecting the
life or character of a man—you can put up with a
decision on financial matters—issuing sentences of
condemnation or preliminary condemnation, putting a man in chains or prison, or torturing him, he
may hold an office in an honorary fashion (*On
Idolatry* 17.2.3).

For Tertullian the practical exigencies of public office present insuperable problems. The role of the magistrate is so
closely tied to idolatry and bloodshed that one can scarcely
imagine a Christian's holding such a position. And with
respect to military service in the lower ranks the case is just
as conclusive.

19.1-3[11] But the question now is whether a member of the
faithful can become a soldier and whether a soldier
can be admitted to the Faith even if he is a member
of the rank and file who are not required to offer
sacrifice or decide capital cases. There can be no
compatibility between an oath made to God and
one made to man, between the standard of Christ
and that of the devil, between the camp of light and
the camp of darkness. The soul cannot be beholden
to two masters, God and Caesar. Moses, to be sure,
carried a rod; Aaron wore a military belt and John
had a breast plate. If one wants to play around with
the topic, Jesus, son of Nun [i.e. Joshua] led an
army and the Jewish nation went to war. But how
will a Christian do so? Indeed how will he serve in
the army even during peacetime without the sword
that Jesus Christ has taken away? Even if soldiers
came to John and got advice on how they ought to
act, even if the centurion became a believer, the
Lord, by taking away Peter's sword, disarmed

[11]Text: CCL 2.1120.

every soldier thereafter. We are not allowed to
wear any uniform that symbolizes a sinful act
(19.1-3).

Tertullian's position here is clear, but the distinctions he
makes and the reasons he gives for his views point to new
developments which were scarcely touched upon by Christian writers up to this point. First, a clear distinction is
made between Christians who sign up for military service
after conversion and those who are converted while in the
army. Tertullian here argues that the distinction is mean-
ingless as far as Christian principles are concerned. By
focusing on soldiers who were below the rank of centurion
and thus not responsible for conducting pagan rites or
carrying out capital punishment (acts which are on their
face immoral), the apologist also indicates that his objections apply not only to those engaged in specific acts of
idolatry or bloodshed but to the soldier who may never
raise his hand in violence. Even in peacetime he must carry
the sword, the symbol of bloodletting, which is inimical to
the law of Christ and which the Christians must have
nothing to do with. Furthermore, the military oath (*sacramentum*) is an affront to the promise (*sacramentum*) made
at baptism, and there is an unbridgeable chasm between
the camp of darkness and the camp of light. A man must
choose between God and Caesar.

Quite clearly other Christians of the time did not see eye
to eye with Tertullian on this issue since they appealed to
examples from both the Old and the New Testament (i.e.
Moses, Aaron, Joshua, John the Baptist, the Centurion
who believed in Christ) as justification for serving in the
army. Tertullian will have none of this. For him Christ's
action in the Garden of Gethsemane settled the matter
beyond doubt. In disarming Peter he disarmed all soldiers,
and, as he says elsewhere, it was on this occasion that Jesus
"cursed the works of the sword for ever after" (*On Patience*
3). Thus, for Christians the military uniform itself is an
insult, and they should have nothing to do with it.

If *On Idolatry* reveals Tertullian as a staunch pacifist, his treatise *On the Crown*, which was written perhaps more than a dozen years later (i.e. ca. 211 A.D.), discusses many of the same issues in greater detail and reflects some slight modification in the apologist's thinking. The occasion for the work was the refusal by a Christian legionnaire to wear the traditional military crown offered to him on the occasion of a celebration honoring the emperor Caracalla's accession to power. Though this action caused consternation among the legionnaire's Christian colleagues in the army, Tertullian defends it as an exceptional act of bravery, and his discourse is an attack on the idolatrous character of the military crown. In chapter eleven, where he takes up the issue of military service itself, he sets forth his ideas at some length.

11.1-7[12] Before treating the matter of a military crown I think we must first ask whether military service is appropriate for Christians at all. What is the point in talking about incidental matters when the assumptions which they rest on are wrong from the start. Do we think that one can rightfully superimpose a human oath on one made to God? and that a man can answer to a second lord once he has acknowledged Christ? and that he can abjure father, mother, and all his neighbors when the Law prescribes that they be honored and loved next to God and the Gospel holds them in the same high esteem, valuing only Christ himself above them? Is it right to make a profession of the sword when the Lord has proclaimed that the man who uses it will perish by it.

Will a son of peace who should not even go to court take part in battle. Will a man who does not avenge wrongs done to himself have any part in chains, prisons, tortures and punishments. Will he perform guard duty for anyone other than Christ, or will he do so on the Lord's day when he is not

[12]Text: CCL 2.1056.

doing it for Christ Himself?" Will he stand guard at the temples which he has forsworn. Will he go to a banquet at places where the apostle disapproves of it? At night will he protect those [demons] that he has exorcised during the day, leaning and resting all the while on the spear that pierced the side of Christ? Will he carry the standards that rival Christ's? Will he ask his commander for a password when he has already received one from God? At the moment of death will he be disturbed by the trumpeter's horn if he looks forward to being awakened by the horn of the angel? Will he be cremated according to the usual practice when this has been forbidden him and when he has been freed by Christ from the punishment of fire? By looking around one can see how many other forms of wrongdoing are involved in fulfilling the duties of military camps, things which must be considered violations of God's law. Carrying the title 'Christian' from the camp of life to the camp of darkness is itself a violation.

The situation is different if the faith comes to a man after he is in the army, as with the soldiers whom John admitted to baptism and the converted centurion whom Christ praised and the one whom Peter instructed in the faith. Nonetheless, once a man has accepted the faith and has been marked with its seal, he must immediately leave the service, as many have done, or he has to engage in all kinds of quibbling to avoid offending God in ways that are forbidden to men even outside the service. Or, finally, he will have to endure for God what civilian members of the faith have been no less willing to accept. Military service offers neither impunity for wrongdoing nor immunity from martyrdom. The Gospel is one and the same for Christians everywhere. Jesus will deny everyone who denies Him and will acknowledge everyone who acknowledges Him. He will save the life that has been given up for his Name's sake but will destroy the one that was saved at the expense of his Name for money's sake. In his eyes the faithful civilian is as much a soldier as the faithful soldier is a civilian. There is no allowance for a plea of necessity. No necessity for wrongdoing is incumbent on those for whom the only necessity is to avoid wrongdoing. Someone, you say, is pressed into sacrificing or officially denying Christ by the inevitability of torture or punishment. All the same, Church discipline does not wink even at that kind of necessity because the necessity to fear denial and to suffer martyrdom is greater than the necessity to avoid martyrdom and to make the required offering. What is more, a pretext like this undercuts the whole meaning of the baptismal oath, thereby opening the door to even voluntary sins. For desire itself could be considered necessity inasmuch as it is a source of compulsion. On the matter of official crowns, I would give the same answer to other arguments that are used to bolster the familiar cry of necessity because we must either refuse offices in order to avoid falling into sin or we must undergo martyrdom in order to be freed from these obligations (11.1-7).

Here Tertullian reviews some of the issues and arguments that he cited in the *On Idolatry* (e.g. the problem of pagan worship, the conflict between the baptismal oath and the military oath, the incompatibility between bloodshed and Christ's words in *Matthew* 26, 52), but he also underscores his point by insisting that the same laws of morality apply to soldiers as to civilians and that necessity is no plea at all for idolatry or denial of the Faith. Thus, Christian civilians must avoid military service altogether. Soldier-converts, however, are in a slightly different position. Although it would be better for them to abandon the service "as many have done", Tertullian seems to acknowledge the possibility of staying in the army provided no act is performed that is contrary to the Faith.

Such a course involves so much quibbling that it seems an impossibility, but Tertullian does not rule it out of court. In short, we have a slight modification of his pacifist views; Christians could remain in the army as long as their role was non-violent.

The reasons for these changes in Tertullian's thinking are not hard to find. We should remember, first, that desertion was a capital offense, and even if a deserter could avoid this punishment, he would still lose his severance pay and all the other benefits that accrued to an individual when he was mustered out of the army. One might be inclined, then, to take with a grain of salt Tertullian's remark that "many" were following this path. What is perhaps more important is the fact that during Septimius Severus' reign (193-211 A.D.) civil offices of the empire were increasingly populated by military personnel. Under such circumstances it was possible for a soldier to spend a whole career in the army without ever doing battle or even engaging in police duty. Also, at this time the number of former slaves and other non-citizens accepted into the service was constantly growing, and it would not be surprising to find Christians joining the army simply to raise their social or financial status. Quite probably many of them were asking themselves what harm there could be in their serving if the prospects for avoiding combat were good, and if they stayed in the lower ranks where they would not have to offer sacrifice or execute prisoners. Such "rationalizing" might explain why the legionnaire praised by Tertullian in the *De Corona* seems to be an exception, why Christians were citing Scripture to justify military service and why Tertullian makes some concessions (begrudging as they are) in this later treatise. He was, in all likelihood, dealing with a trend that was quite irreversible.

This interpretation is supported by what we find in a contemporary document known as the *Apostolic Tradition*, which is attributed to Hippolytus of Rome. It provides a list of Church rites and practices in that city during the early decades of the third century A.D., and, among other things, it prescribes how a Christian soldier should conduct himself. Canon XVI of this document reads in part as follows:

XVI[13] A soldier in the lower ranks shall kill no one. If ordered to do so, he shall not obey, and he shall not take an oath. If he does not want to comply with this directive, let him be dismissed [i.e. from the Church]. If anyone exercises the power of the sword or is a civil magistrate who wears the purple, let him give up the office or be dismissed. A catechumen or a member of the faithful who wants to join the army should be dismissed because he has shown contempt for God.

With respect to Christians already in the army a distinction is made here between common soldiers on the one hand and officers and magistrates on the other. The former are not required to desert as long as they avoid bloodshed, and the prohibition against taking human life is so absolute that it could even require disobedience to a direct command from a superior. Those in the higher ranks, who are immediately responsible for issuing capital sentences or carrying them out, need to give up their responsibilities since they cannot avoid wrongdoing. A civilian who wants to join the army and thereby voluntarily put himself in extreme peril of sin has by that very fact put himself outside the pale of the Christian community.

The author of this document is trying to wrestle with two facts: the great danger to the faith that a military career entailed and the obvious presence of Christians in the army. The very existence of the Canon probably indicates that a growing number of men were somehow finding army life compatible with Christianity, and an absolute requirement that they desert was out of the question. Thus, the concession to them in this document was quite precise. How workable such arrangements were in actual practice we have little way of knowing, but the prohibition at the end against volunteering reveals that the Church in Rome was still throwing all its weight behind efforts to discourage Christians from having anything to do with the service.

[13]Text: SC 11².72.

3. St. Cyprian of Carthage (died 258 A.D.)

The strength and longevity of such efforts must remain a question. We do know, however, that Cyrpian of Carthage, Tertullian's successor as the most prominent African Christian writer, neither dealt with the issue head-on, nor, it seems, did he provide the kind of clear-cut response that the apologist did. It is true that he decries homicide (*On the Dress of Virgins* 11), that he criticises the vanity of military life (*To Donatus* 11) and that he is not fooled when reasons of state are used to veil the horrors of war. In fact, on this latter issue he makes an important point that will subsequently reappear in Lactantius' pacifist remarks. Commenting on the general economic and social decline in the empire of his day, he says, in his *To Donatus*:

> 6.[14] Notice that the roads have been made impassable by robbers, the seas have been filled with pirates, and everywhere wars have broken out with the ghastly bloodletting of the camp. The world is drenched with mutual bloodshed. When individuals slay a man, it is a crime. When killing takes place on behalf of the state, it is called a virtue. Crimes go unpunished not because the perpetrators are said to be guiltless but because their cruelty is so extensive (*To Donatus* 6).

Thus, Cyprian rejects a double standard for private and public morality in this area, and elsewhere he suggests that there is an inherent conflict between acts of violence and the celebration of the Christian mysteries. Addressing himself specifically to Christians, he insists that "after the reception of the Eucharist the hand is not to be stained with the sword and bloodshed" (*On the Goodness of Patience* 14).

It must be admitted, however, that Cyprian never goes beyond the general tenor of these statements, and his opposition has to be weighed against other remarks scattered

[14]Text: CCL 3A.6.

throughout his works. He seems to feel that wars are inevitable (*On Mortality* 2); he argues that the contemporary decline in military forces within the Empire is one of the many signs of God's punishment (*To Demetrianus* 3 and 17), and he prays for the success of the imperial armies in warding off enemies.

> 20.[15] Only when we go to God will we receive the promised rewards. Nonetheless, we always pray that enemies be kept at bay, that rains be granted, and that adversities either be taken away or mitigated; day and night we pour out our supplications beseeching and placating God, earnestly and continually pleading with him for your safety and peace (*To Demetrianus* 20).

We have seen in Tertullian and the Greek apologists that commonplace sentiments like these must not be taken as endorsing Christian participation in military action against the empire's enemies. In the absence of direct evidence, however, we should be cautious about putting Cyprian in the pacifist camp, especially in light of his profuse use of military metaphors for the Christian life. In this connection he does not hesitate to say, for example, that "It is the task of a good soldier to defend the camp against traitors and enemies of the emperor. It is the task of a glorious leader to preserve the standards entrusted to him" (Epistle 73.10). And in describing man's ultimate destiny, he uses a military analogy that is hard to reconcile with trenchant pacifism: "If it is a glorious thing for soldiers in the world to return home in triumph to their native land after defeating the enemy, how much more impressive and glorious is man's triumphant return to paradise following the devil's defeat" (*To Fortunatus* 13).

Statements like these, when coupled with the admiration which he expresses elsewhere for certain soldier-martyrs (*Epistle* 39.3) make it difficult to suppose that Cyprian considered all forms of armed conflict immoral. What is

[15]Text: CCL 3A.47.

more likely is that the question of war and military service was never a pressing issue for him. Like other Christian writers of the pre-Constantinian era, he condemns bloodshed and reinforces traditional ideas about the peaceful character of Christianity, but at the same time he acknowledges that the empire cannot survive without military force. How these two necessities are reconciled he seems not to have considered. His position is one more indication that for many people the whole issue of the Christians' position on war and military service remained rather ambiguous, and that there was no easy solution to the problem of rendering service both to God and to Caesar.

4. Clement of Alexandria (c. 150—c. 215 A.D.)

Much the same can be said for Tertullian's Greek contemporary, Clement of Alexandria, a theologian of stature who was much concerned with the integration of pagan and Christian culture. Like Athenagoras before him Clement thinks of wars as being inspired by demons (i.e. pagan deities) (*Exhortation to the Greeks* III.42.1), and he makes the point more than once that Christians are "a peaceful race." "In peace, not in war are we trained," he says in *The Teacher* (1.12.99), and later in the same work he uses the imagery of music to describe man as a "peaceful instrument" who honors God with "the word of peace alone" (*The Teacher* 2.4.42). Elsewhere, following the lead of St. Paul, he uses military analogies to explain the Christians' call to grace and their role in the bloodless army of Christ.

XI.116[16]   When the blaring trumpet sounds, it calls the troops together and proclaims war. Will not Christ Himself who has played a melody of peace to the very ends of the earth, gather together his own soldiers of peace? He did, indeed, o man, assemble a bloodless army

[16]Text: SC 2.184.

by means of his blood and his word, and to that
army he entrusted the Kingdom of Heaven. Christ's
trumpet is his gospel. He blew it, and we heard. Let
us put on the armor of peace 'donning the breastplate of integrity' and taking up 'the shield of faith'
and putting on 'the helmet of salvation'. Let us whet
'the sword of the spirit which is the word of God'
(*Ephes.* 6.14-17; *Thess.* 5.8). In this fashion does the
Apostle arrange us in the battleline of peace. Armed
with invulnerable weapons like these, let us take our
position against the evil one (*Exhortation to the
Greeks* XI.116-7).

General statements like these, however, must be weighed
against others which, if they do not actually endorse Christian participation in war, are difficult to reconcile very easily
with an absolute rejection of violence. Thus Clement does
not hesitate to praise Moses as a military commander (*Miscellanies* 1.24.162), to acknowledge the appropriateness of
certain military practices in the Old Testament (*ibid* 2.18.82)
and to approve the Jews' despoiling the Egyptians on the
grounds that it was the usual practice in war or a legitimate
means of seeking reparation (ibid. 1.23.157). One could
argue, of course, that all these examples say nothing about
the requirments of the New Dispensation, but even in this
context it is hard to imagine that the military profession
itself created much embarrassment to Clement. Referring to
Luke 3.14 he says without further comment that Christ
"through the mouth of John commands soldiers to be content with their wages and nothing more" (*The Teacher*
3.12.91); with an approving eye he compares Christians to
warriors (*Miscellanies* 6.14.112) and Christ to the military
commander who "directs his troops on the line with an eye
to their safety" (*The Teacher 1.7.54*). He says that Christians
honor the martyrs just as the Hellenes honored those who
had fallen in battle (*Miscellanies* 4.4.14), and when he
speaks of the spiritual destiny that all men are called to,
those in the military profession are not excluded.

X.100[17] It is man's very nature to be on intimate terms with God. We do not compel the horse to plow or the bull to engage in the hunt, but direct each animal to the kind of work most natural to it; in the same way we call upon man, who is truly a heavenly creature and who has been made for the vision of heaven, to come to a knowledge of God. Laying hold of what is intimately and peculiarly his own as distinct from other living things, we advise him to outfit himself with godliness as an adequate preparation for his eternal journey. If you are a farmer, we say, till the earth, but acknowledge the God of farmers; if you love seafaring, sail on, but remember to call upon the celestial Helmsman. If you were in the army when you were seized by the knowledge of God, obey the Commander who gives just commands (*Exhortation to the Greeks* X.100.2).

The point here is that whatever a man's role in life may be, he should look beyond the demands of the moment to his eternal destiny. It would appear that Clement no more expected the Christian soldier to abandon his profession than he expected the farmer or the sailor to do so, and it seems safe to conclude that the Alexandrian writer would not follow Tertullian in claiming that military service and Christian faith are mutually exclusive.

5. Origen (c. 185 — c. 254 A.D.)

Such was not the case, however, with his pupil Origen, who was the Church's most brilliant biblical scholar and most profound theologian in the pre-Constantinian era. Origen took strong exception to any Christian involvement in war, and more than any other writer of the period he candidly faced the problems created by this issue, and he spelled out some of the implications of the pacifist position.

[17]Text: SC 2.168.

His views on the subject are contained for the most part in the treatise *Against Celsus*, an apologetic piece which was composed around 248 A.D. and which was intended, as we saw above, as a refutation of charges leveled against Christians by the pagan critic Celsus more than half a century earlier. Celsus, as we have noted, viewed the worship of Caesar and the defense of the empire as inseparable elements in any loyal citizen's concern for the realm, and he claimed that if all Romans followed the Christian pattern of refusing divine honors to the ruler they would expose the empire to the ravages of "the most lawless and uncivilized barbarians." Origen's view of what would happen under such circumstances is quite the opposite:

8.68[18]   Indeed let everyone do the same as I in rejecting the Homeric teaching [i.e. that the god Kronos confers temporal power] but preserving the notion of the divine right of the emperor and obeying the injunction, 'Honor the king' (1 *Peter* 2.17). If this were to happen, the emperor would not be 'left alone or be deserted and earthly affairs be in the hands of the most lawless and uncivilized barbarians.' If, as Celsus says, everybody followed my lead, it is clear that the barbarians themselves, once converted to God's word, would become most law-abiding and civilized. All cults would be done away with and only the Christians' would survive. Someday Christianity will be the only cult because the Word is ceaselessly conquering more and more souls (*Against Celsus* 8.68).

In a sense this statement is no answer at all to Celsus' objections since the conversion of the barbarians is hardly in the offing, and Origen's suggestion that the spread of Christianity would make war against Rome's neighbors obsolete is not a self-evident truth. Nonetheless, what the Christian writer is arguing here is that the rejection of pagan worship involves a redefinition of loyalty to Rome rather than a

[18]Text: SC 150.332.

diminution of it, and throughout his writings it is obvious that Origen recognizes the need for temporal power in the created world. In fact, he follows Melito and Tertullian in claiming that the rule of Augustus was a providential means of facilitating the spread of the Gospel.

2.30[19]   It is well known that Jesus was born in the reign of Augustus, who, one might say, brought the mass of mankind under a single sovereignty. The existence of many kingdoms would have hindered the spread of Jesus' teaching over the whole world not only for the reasons already cited but because everywhere men would have been forced to serve in the army and to go to war on behalf of their country. . . . How could this peaceful teaching, which prohibits a man from avenging himself even against his enemies, have gained sway if the whole world situation at the time of Jesus had not been made more peaceful (*Against Celsus* 2.30).

But if the need for a peaceful empire is acknowledged, then Celsus' question about the Christians' contributions to its safety and well-being only become more acute. Origen seems to recognize this fact when he takes up the specific issue of Christians serving in the army.

8.73[20]   Celsus goes on to encourage us 'to assist the emperor with all our strength, to work with him on just undertakings, to fight for him and to serve in his army, if he requires it, either as a soldier or a general.' To this we should reply that when the occasion arises, we provide the emperors with divine assistance, as it were, by putting on the 'armor of God' (*Ephesians* 6.11). We do so in obedience to the voice of the Apostle who says 'My advice is that first and foremost you offer prayers, supplications, petitions and thanksgiving for all men, especially for the

[19]Text: SC 132.360.
[20]Text: SC 150.344.

emperors, and all those in authority' (I *Timothy* 2.1-2). To be sure, the more pious a man is the more effectively does he assist the emperors—more so than the troops that go out and kill as many of the enemy as possible on the battleline. This would be our answer to those who are strangers to our faith and who ask us to take up arms and to kill men for the common good. Even in your religion priests attached to certain images and guardians of temples which are dedicated to what you believe are gods should keep their right hand undefiled for sacrifice so as to make their usual offerings to beings that you consider deities with hands that are free of blood and murder. And, of course, in war time you do not enlist your priests. If this is a reasonable procedure, how much more so is it for Christians to fight as priests and worshippers of God while others fight as soldiers. Though they keep their right hands clean, the Christians fight through their prayers to God on behalf of those doing battle in a just cause and on behalf of an emperor who is ruling justly in order that all opposition and hostility toward those who are acting rightly may be eliminated. What is more, by overcoming with our prayers all the demons who incite wars, who violate oaths and who disturb the peace we help emperors more than those who are supposedly doing the fighting... We do not go out on the campaign with him [i.e. the emperor] even if he insists, but we do battle on his behalf by raising a special army of piety through our petitions to God (*Against Celsus* 8.73).

This passage establishes some important principles and raises several interesting questions. In taking what could be described as a bifocal view, Origen first acknowledges the possibility of just wars and the role they play in protecting the empire from external threats. This is a point he had touched on earlier in this treatise (4.82) where he suggested that the life and activities of the bees were a lesson to man that "if wars are ever necessary, they ought to be just and ordered." For Origen, however, it is also evident that pagans and Christians have quite distinct responsibilities in their joint concern for the safety and wellbeing of the empire. If placing the whole Christian community in the same category as that of pagan priesthoods must have appeared absurd to non-Christian contemporaries, that fact underscores the difference between Origen's outlook on the problem and theirs. The need for defending the empire's borders was real, but it was not the only reality. In Origen's scheme of things Christians are, "the entering wedge of the eschatological kingdom" (Caspary 128), and because their role in society is to work toward that kingdom, warfare for them has become spiritualized. Their battle is against the powers of evil both within and outside man that stir up conflicts and prevent a lasting peace. Christian service to the empire, then, must be in the realm of the spirit or not at all.

Celsus had made the point that in refusing to take up arms the Christians were not being consistent because they themselves had originated in a revolt of dissident Jews. In denying this charge Origen shows that for himself, at least, Christian pacifism is based not on the issue of idolatry or the moral excesses of military life but quite simply on Christ's prohibition against killing.

> 3.8[21]   The assertion that 'certain Jews at the time of Christ revolted against the Jewish community and followed Jesus' is not less false than the claim 'that the Jews had their origin in a revolt of certain Egyptians.' Celsus and those who agree with him will not be able to cite a single act of rebellion on the part of the Christians. If a revolt had indeed given rise to the Christian community, if Christians took their origin from the Jews, who were allowed to take up arms in defense of their possessions and to kill their enemies, the Christian Lawgiver would not have made homicide absolutely forbidden. He would not have

[21]Text: SC 136.26.

taught that his disciples were never justified in taking such action against a man even if he were the
greatest wrongdoer. [Jesus] considered it contrary
to his divinely inspired legislation to approve any
kind of homicide whatsoever. If Christians had
started with a revolt, they would never have submit-
ted to the kind of peaceful laws which permitted
them to be slaughtered 'like sheep' (*Ps.* 44.11) and
which made them always incapable of taking vengeance on their persecutors because they followed
the law of gentleness and love (*Against Celsus* 3.8).

And, later in the same work, he echoes the words of Isaiah in
reiterating this point.

5.33[22] To those who ask about our origin and our founder
we reply that we have come in response to Jesus'
commands to beat into plowshares the rational
swords of conflict and arrogance and to change into
pruning hooks those spears that we used to fight
with. For we no longer take up the sword against
any nation, nor do we learn the art of war any more.
Instead of following the traditions that made us
'strangers to the covenants' (*Ephes.* 2.12), we have
become sons of peace through Jesus our founder
(5.33).

Origen was well aware, of course, that Christian pacifism
was a marked departure from Jewish practice, and he
wrestled with the question of how to interpret the divinely
sanctioned wars of Israel. He solved the problem by appealing both to history and to allegory.

7.26[23] Denying to the Jews of old, who had their own
socio-political system and their own territory, the
right to march against their enemies, to wage war in
order to protect their traditions, to kill, or to impose
some kind of punishment on adulterers, murderers

[22]Text: SC 147.98.
[23]Text: SC 150.72.

and others who committed similar crimes would
have been nothing short of consigning them to complete destruction when an enemy attacked their
nation because their own Law would have sapped
their strength and would have forestalled their resistance. But Providence, which in an earlier time gave
us the Law and now has given us the Gospel of Jesus
Christ, did not want the Jewish system perpetuated
and so destroyed the city of the Jews and their
temple along with the divine worship that was celebrated there through sacrifices and prescribed rites
(*Against Celsus* 7.26).

Here the ethical change effected by the Gospel is explained
in historical and political terms. The demise of the auto-
nomous Jewish state removed the need for physical force
among God's people, who were, in any case, no longer to be
identified with a particular nation. Under an interim peace
established by Rome they could now work toward the goal
of universal peace without the weapons of war. Whatever
coercive methods were needed to keep the barbarians at bay
could be entrusted to the armies of Rome, but for Christians
the New Dispensation absolutely forbade violence. When
Peter cut off Malchus' ear in the Garden of Gethsemane
(*Matthew* 26.51), he demonstrated that he had not taken the
peace of the Lord to heart but was still operating within the
Old Testament context (*Commentariorum Series* 101). For
Origen the obvious meaning of Christ's warning about per-
ishing by the sword is that "we must beware of unsheathing
the sword simply because we are in the army or for the sake
of avenging private injuries or under any other pretext
because Christ's teaching in the Gospels considers all of
these uses an abomination. . . . If, then, we must be peaceful
toward those who despise peace, we must use the sword
against no man" (*ibid.* 102). It is notable here that service in
the army as such is not excluded, but at the same time it is no
excuse at all for taking human life. This approach follows
the lines of what we have already seen in the *Canon of
Hippolytus* and in Tertullian's *On the Crown*. Thus, what

seems to be developing in this period is an acknowledgment by pacifist writers that Christians may serve in the army provided they have nothing to do with bloodshed.

Elsewhere in his writings Origen appeals to allegory as a way of understanding passages from the Old Testament that seem to endorse acts of violence. Thus, for example, he says that it is impossible to interpret literally God's promise to the Jews that they would slay all their enemies (*Against Celsus* 7.19), and he argues that when the psalmist says, "Every morning I killed all the sinners on earth..." (*Ps.* 101.8), he is to be understood as referring to the destruction of the "fleshly desire" and of all "thoughts and desires that are opposed to the truth" (*ibid.* 7.22). In his *Homilies on Joshua* Origen states quite specifically that wars of the Old Testament must have a spiritual sense if they are to be incorporated into the Christian scheme of things.

> XV[24] Unless those carnal wars [i.e. of the Old Testament] were a symbol of spiritual wars, I do not think that the Jewish historical books would ever have been passed down by the Apostles to be read by Christ's followers in their churches...Thus, the Apostle, being aware that physical wars are no longer to be waged by us but that our struggles are to be only battles of the soul against spiritual adversaries, gives orders to the soldiers of Christ like a military commander when he says, 'Put on the armor of God so as to be able to hold your ground against the wiles of the devil' (*Ephes.* 6.11) (XV.1).

Whether Origen views Old Testament wars as something which has been abrogated by historical developments or whether he sees them as containing a spiritual message for Christians, there is no doubt where he stands on the issue of Christians and violence. What is more important, he is the first Christian writer to treat in some detail the problems created by pacifism both within the Scriptural tradition of the Church itself, and in the relations that the Christian

[24]Text: SC 71.330.

community had with the pagan world around it. If his notion that Old Testament violence was made obsolete by the commands of Christ did not win general acceptance in subsequent ages, the questions he raised and the answers he gave on the whole issue of war and military service could not be ignored. If his concept of loyalty to the state was too spiritual for both pagans and Christians, and if his expectations about the effectiveness of Christian prayer in the development of a wholly peaceful empire seemed naive (Origen himself came to have some doubt about the latter, at least in the world of time [cf. *Against Celsus* 8.72]), he at least wrestled with the real issues, and he fashioned a kind of ideal that would live long after him. He was, in fact, the most articulate and eloquent pacifist in the early Christian Church.

6. Arnobius (died c. 330 A.D.)

In the period before Constantine the two remaining figures who had something to say about war and the Christian conscience are Arnobius and Lactantius, both of whom wrote in the early decades of the fourth century. Arnobius' comments exhibit a certain amount of ambivalence on the subject although most of his remarks reflect pacifist sentiments. He reaffirms the principle that for a Christian "it is not right to repay evil for evil; it is better to suffer an injury than to inflict one and to shed one's own blood rather than pollute one's hands and one's conscience with the blood of another" (*Against the Pagans* 1.6), and he claims that this teaching has actually brought about a decline of bloodshed in society. He criticizes the wars by which Rome exterminated some nations and made others subject to her yoke (2.1), and in his attacks on pagan worship he finds a natural target in the God of War who "piles the battlefields high with corpses, creates torrents of blood, overturns the most stable empires, reduces cities to rubble, subjects free men to slavery, and takes delight in such things as civil conflict, the mutual slaughter of brothers going to their death together, and finally, the horror of father and son killing each other" (3.26). On the other hand, Arnobius defends Christians against the charge of bringing calamities on the Empire by arguing along different lines. With at least some degree of satisfaction he claims that during the three hundred years of Christianity's existence, "there were countless victories over conquered enemies, the empire's boundaries were expanded, and nations which had never been heard of were brought under our control" (1.14). Though this latter point is scarcely an endorsement of Christian participation in war, and it could be argued that Arnobius is adopting Origen's bifocal view on the issue, there is no indication of such in his writing. Amid all the tendentious statements in his work we are left with the general impression that he could not reconcile Christian principles with participation in war but that he never seriously wrestled with the problem.

7. *Lactantius (c. 240 — c. 320 A.D.)*

The same is not true of his pupil Lactantius, who had considerably more to say on the issue and who may be considered a kind of transitional figure in the history of the problem because his own change in outlook reflects a change in the Christian community at large. Throughout most of his *Divine Institutes* (a work composed between 304-311 A.D. and intended to explain Christianity to the educated public of the day) he has nothing but harsh words for any form of bloodshed. Commenting on Cicero's advice that a good man should not inflict injury unless he is injured himself, Lactantius suggests that an individual who does so loses the name "good" because "it is no less evil to return an injury than it is to inflict one" (*Divine Institutes* 6.18.17; cf. 6.18.25, 29-32). Like Athenagoras during the second century he criticizes the gladiatorial combats on the grounds that it is wrong "not only to take part in slaughter but to be present and to observe those who are so engaged" (*Div. Inst.* 5.17.13), and he presses this point without ambiguity:

6.20.9[25]   We must avoid them [i.e. the shows] because they
are a strong enticement to vice, and they have an
immense capacity for corrupting souls. Rather than
contributing something to a happy life they are, in
fact, exceedingly harmful. For anybody who finds it
pleasurable to watch a man being slain (however
justly the person was condemned) has violated his
own conscience as much as if he had been a specta-
tor and participant in a clandestine murder. The
actual term used by the pagans for these events in
which human blood is spilled is 'games.' They are so
alienated from their own humanity that they believe
they are playing when they take human lives. In fact,
however, the perpetrators are more harmful than all
those people whose blood is a source of delight to
them. I ask, then, whether anyone can be just and
reverent if he not only permits men who are facing
imminent death and are pleading for mercy to be
slain but also flogs his victims and brings death
through cruel and inhuman punishments whenever
he finds himself unsated by the wounds already
inflicted or by the blood already spilled (*Div. Inst.*
6.20.9-12).

The same criticism is applied in the public realm when
Lactantius follows Arnobius in condemning the bloody
wars of Rome's history and when he opposes both military
service and capital punishment.

6.20.15[26]   It is not right for those who are striving to stay on
the path of virtue to become associated with this
kind of wholesale slaughter [i.e. of the gladiatorial
combats] or to take part in it. For when God forbids
killing, he is not only ordering us to avoid armed
robbery, which is contrary even to public law, but
He is forbidding what men regard as ethical. Thus, it
is not right for a just man to serve in the army since

[25]Text; CSEL 19.557.
[26]Text: CSEL 19.558.

justice itself is his form of service. Nor is it right for a just man to charge someone with a capital crime. It does not matter whether you kill a man with the sword or with a word since it is killing itself that is prohibited. And so there must be no exception to this command of God. Killing a human being whom God willed to be inviolable, is always wrong (*Div. Inst.* 6.20.15-17).

This is pacifism pure and simple. It should be noted that Lactantius makes no distinction between peacetime and wartime service in the army. For him it is all of a piece. The Roman spirit of reverence (*pietas*), he says, is found "among those who have nothing to do with war, who preserve a spirit of peace with everyone, who are friendly even with their enemies, who love all men as their brothers, and who know how to control their anger and to temper their wrath with a tranquil spirit" (*Div. Inst.* 5.10.10).

The notion that it is a virtue to fight for the advantages that will accrue to one's own country rests, Lactantius claims, on a false premise. "For the advantages to your country are nothing but disadvantages to another state or nation. Such things as expanding one's territory with lands taken by violence from another nation, increasing the size of the empire and raising the amount of revenue one receives are certainly not virtues but their opposite" (*Div. Inst.* 5.6.19). Lactantius goes on to say that people who claim to benefit their country in this way do not know either what the term "benefit" or what the term "justice" means.

6.6[27] How can a man be just if he harms, hates, robs or kills? Those who strive to benefit their country do all of these things. They do not know what the term 'benefit' means if they think that only something which can be held in the hand is useful or beneficial....Whoever endows his country with these so-called blessings, that is, who ever fills the treasury

[27]Text: CSEL 19.503.

with money by conquering states and killing people, whoever captures territory and makes his fellow citizens richer is exalted to the skies and thought to possess the highest virtue. It is not only ignorant people who make this mistake but even philosophers who set the guidelines for injustice so as not to leave foolishness and malice without an ordered structure and foundation. Thus, when they discuss the obligations connected with military affairs, none of their remarks has to do with justice or virtue in the proper sense"...(*Div. Inst.* 6.6.22-24).

It is precisely this lack of justice which Lactantius later criticizes in Rome's wars of expansion ("How far removed expediency is from justice the Roman people themselves demonstrate. They have taken possession of the whole world by declaring war through the Fetiales, by legally inflicting injuries and by seizing or robbing others' possessions" [*Div. Inst.* 6.9.4]), and he follows Cyprian's lead in decrying the way in which the magnitude of an act puts the stamp of approval on wrongdoing.

1.18.8[28] [The Romans] think the only path to immortality is that of leading armies, devastating foreign territories, leveling cities, destroying towns and killing free men or subjecting them to slavery. The more men they beat up, rob or kill, the more distinguished and famous they think they are. Captivated by the vision of empty glory they call their criminal acts virtue. It would be better, I think, for them to fashion their concept of deity from the slaughter of wild animals than to accept such a bloody kind of immortality. If a man throttles a single individual, he is considered a vile criminal and people think it wrong to allow him to enter the earthly dwellings of the gods. But a man who has killed countless thousands, has made the fields run with blood and has polluted rivers is

[28]Text: CSEL 19.68.

admitted not only into the temples but into heaven itself (*Div. Inst.* 1.18.8-10).

For Lactantius the only means of correcting this concept of heroism and virtue and of bringing an end to wars is the worship of the one true God: "But if the one God were worshipped, there would be no dissension or wars because men would recognize that they are sons of the one God and thus bound together by a holy and inviolable bond of divine kinship. There would be no intrigues since they would know what kind of punishments God, who is aware of hidden crimes and even a man's thoughts, had in store for those who took human life..." (*Div. Inst.* 5.8.6). On this point Lactantius is not very far from the hopes of Origen although the latter's concept of assisting the empire's army with prayers is wholly outside his ken. In all Lactantius' early work, at least, it would appear that violence and war is one issue on which pagans and Christians are hopelessly divided.

In works written after the rise of Constantine, however, the Christian apologist seems less certain about that point. In the *Epitome* of the *Divine Institutes*, for example, he makes a comment about the distinction between virtue and vice which is quite revealing. Commenting on the role of the passions in man's life he remarks,

> 56.3[29] These things which God in his wisdom has instilled in man are not evil in themselves. They become so through improper use but are by nature good because they have been given to us for preserving life. Just as courage is good if you are fighting for your country but evil if you are rebelling against it, so too, with the emotions. If you use them for good ends, they will be virtues; if for evil ends, they will be called vices (*Epitome* 56.3-4).

These words suggest that a change has occurred in Lactantius' thinking and that some types of armed conflict are now quite acceptable to him. If so, we can understand why the

[29]Text: CSEL 19.739.

section of the *Epitome* (59.5) dealing with the precept "Thou shalt not kill" says nothing about participating in war although the full text of the *Divine Institutes* is very specific in condemning such actions. A change of this kind is also consonant with Lactantius' attitude toward certain political and military events of the time. In praising Licinius' victory over Maximinus in 313 A.D., for example, the author construes the event as a conflict between Christian and pagan forces, and he is quite confident about God's role in Licinius' victory:

> 46.1[30] With the armies approaching one another, it became evident that an engagement would take place shortly. At this juncture Maximinus made a vow to Jupiter that if he won he would blot out and utterly destroy the name of Christians. On the next night an angel of God appeared to Licinius in his sleep telling him to get up right away and with his entire army to offer prayers to the all high God. If he did that, the victory would be his. Licinius dreamed that when he got up in response to these words, the angel stood at his side and told him how to pray and what words to use. When he woke up, Licinius called for his secretary and dictated to him the words he had heard: 'All High God, we beseech you; Holy God, we beseech you. To you we completely entrust our just cause; to you we entrust our safety; to you we entrust our empire. Through you we have life; through you we are victorious and blessed. All High and Holy God, hear our prayers; we stretch forth our arms to you. Hear us, O Holy, All High God' (*On The Death of the Persecutors.* 46.1-7).

We might discount a passage like this as a piece of rhetorical exaggeration that does little to undermine Lactantius' pacifist position, were it not for the accolades that he heaps on Constantine for the latter's victory over Maxentius in the famous battle of the Milvian Bridge (312 A.D.). He recounts

[30]Text: SC 39.129.

the story of Constantine's dream in which the emperor was instructed to put the sign of Christ on the soldiers' shields (*Death of the Pers.* 44.5.6), and in the manner of Old Testament writers he celebrates the subsequent victory as God's own triumph.

> 52.4[31] With great rejoicing, then, let us celebrate the triumph of God; let us extol the victory of the Lord; day and night let us pour out our prayers in rejoicing; let us pray that he establish forever the peace that has been granted to his people after ten years (*Death of the Pers.* 52.4).

And there is more. Not only is Constantine praised for his military prowess (*Death of the Pers.* 18.10), but in a laudatory passage of the *Divine Institutes* (a passage which seems to have been appended more than a decade after 312 A.D.) the emperor is looked upon as the vice-gerent of the one true God in punishing wrongdoers and restoring justice to the earth.

> 1.1.13[32] Now we take up our task under your auspices, O Constantine, greatest of emperors, the first of Roman princes to cast aside error and to acknowledge and honor the majesty of the one true God. For when that most happy day dawned all over the world, when the all high God raised you to the heights of power, you inaugurated your rule— desirable and beneficial as it is to all men—with a noble beginning. You brought back justice, which had been overturned and blotted out, and you expiated the horrible crimes of other rulers. For this accomplishment God will grant you success, courage and length of days so that even when you are advanced in years, you may continue to direct the helm of state with the same justice with which you commenced your rule as a young man, and you may pass on to your children that responsibility for pro-

[31]Text: SC 39.138.
[32]Text: CSEL 19.4

tecting Rome's name which you received from your Father. On those who continue to afflict the just in other parts of the world that same omnipotent Father will wreak vengeance for their wrong doing. The more delayed that vengeance is the more severe it will be, for just as He is a most indulgent Father toward good men, so, too, is he a very strict judge toward the wicked. In my desire to see to it that God be revered and worshipped, whom should I call upon, whom should I speak to but the man who has restored justice and wisdom to human affairs (*Div. Inst.* 1.1.13-16).

Even a cursory reading of this passage is enough to indicate how different the atmosphere was in which the Christians now found themselves. If they had never been adamantly opposed to temporal power and had, in fact, claimed for themselves a particular kind of loyalty to Rome, they hardly expected to be living under a ruler who was God's own agent in defending the name of Rome, avenging wrongdoing and restoring "justice and wisdom to human affairs." In such a context it was difficult for the Christians to look with a disapproving eye on Constantine's victories over the Church's persecutors even if those triumphs involved bloodshed. Henceforth, the practice of actively opposing all forms of war and military service or of supporting a just conflict only through prayers and ascetic practices would not suffice. The pacifist position which had been the more articulate and, as far as we can tell, the more typical response to the question of war and military service now became a minority view while the unarticulated arguments of non-pacifists began to be spelled out in greater detail.

8. Christian Practices

Before discussing these developments, however, it will be useful to consider what the sources tell us about Christian practice in regard to military service in the period before Constantine. On this score the evidence is neither as extensive nor as explicit as what we have seen thus far, but it provides at least a glimpse into the day-to-day handling of the problem. It also bears witness to the fact that there was division on this issue among the Christians in practice as well as in theory. Except for the few references to soldier-converts in the New Testament we have no evidence for Christians serving in the army prior to the reign of Marcus Aurelius (161-180 A.D.). As we have seen, however, it was at this time that both Celsus' complaint about the Christians' unwillingness to serve and the story about the role of Christian troops in the *Legio XII fulminata* appeared in our sources. Toward the end of the century we have Tertullian's remark that Christians filled the camps of the empire (*Apology* 37.4), and if this claim is surely an exaggeration, it at least indicates that Christians in the army did not go unnoticed. The apologist's comments at the beginning of *On the Crown* (1.1) further suggest that not all Christian soldiers felt compelled to refuse the military crown, and Tertullian's stern advice about service in the army would have had little point if the number of Christians enrolled during his time were insignificant.

About fifty years later Cyprian of Carthage (*Letter* 39.3) records that a confessor in the time of Decius' persecution (250-51 A.D.) had two military uncles who had suffered martyrdom, and Eusebius (*Ecclesiastical History* 6.41.16-22) tells us that several Christian soldiers at Alexandria were executed during an outbreak of violence against the Church there around 249 A.D. The numerical growth of Christians in the army during the second half of the third century is attested by the fact that Diocletian made them the first object of his persecution in 303 A.D. (cf. Eusebius, *Eccl. History* 8.1.7; 8.4.2-3; Lactantius, *On the Death of the Persecutors* 11.3). In fact, Lactantius gives us an interesting account of an event which preceded this action by many months and which reveals some of the problems that were arising during these years.

10.1-4[33] When Diocletian was in the East he made it a practice of sacrificing sheep and examining their livers
for signs of the future because fear led him to be a
diviner of such things. On one occasion in the course
of the sacrifice certain members of the faithful who
were present signed their foreheads with the immor-
tal sign. At this the demons took flight, and the
ritual was thrown into disorder. The diviners were
upset they did not see the usual signs in the entrails,
and they kept repeating the sacrifice, as if they had
gotten unfavorable omens. Again and again the
slain animals gave no sign until finally Tagis the
chief diviner, either because he suspected something
or had seen something, claimed that the victims
were providing no answer because non-believers
were present at the rites. At that point the emperor
became enraged and ordered not only those present
at the rites but everybody in the palace to offer
sacrifice. Anyone who refused was to be scourged,
and the emperor had letters sent out to his commanders ordering troops even in the lower ranks to
be compelled to sacrifice under pain of dismissal for
refusing (*Death of the Pers.* 10.1-4).

Thus, Christians were to be found not only among the
troops most closely associated with the emperor but sufficiently scattered throughout the legions to warrant the
emperor's sending instructions to his commanders concerning them. What is more, a few years later in Armenia at the
eastern end of the empire we are told in rather matter-of-fact
terms that Christians went to war against Maximin Dia
when he attempted to impose pagan practices on them
(*Eusebius, Ecclesiastical History* 9.8.2 and 4).

Inscriptional evidence for the presence of Christians in
the army during the pre-Constantine era is meager in the
extreme. Although hundreds of epitaphs on soldiers' tombs
have been identified as Christian, only nine or ten of these

[33]Text: SC 39.88.

(the majority of which are from Rome) can be dated in the period before Constantine. Included in these latter is one to a bishop of Laodicea in Phrygia which records with pride his service in Pisidia prior to being elevated to the episcopacy. Apparently his military career did not create any scandal. In his case, as well as in all similar ones, the real significance of the epitaphs is that the communities in which these men were buried did not forbid such references on the tombs, nor, apparently, did they reject the military profession as incompatible with Christianity.

9. *The Military Martyrs*

There is another side of the issue, however, which is reflected in the trials of several soldier-martyrs who went to their deaths during the third and early fourth centuries because they refused to enlist or stay in the army. Although the *Acts* of these Martyrs have to be evaluated with great care, they provide valuable insights into the problems faced by at least some Christians during the period before Constantine when they attempted to serve both God and Caesar.

The first individual of this kind about whom we have any detailed information is Marinus, a legionnaire stationed in Palestine, who was beheaded ca. 260 A.D. On the eve of being promoted to the rank of centurion he was denounced by a rival as being unfit for the honor "because he was a Christian and would not offer sacrifice to the emperors" (*Martyrdom of St. Marinus* 10-11). Although given a chance to recant, he persisted in his belief and was executed. The short account of Marinus' trial in the *Acts* is important because it tends to substantiate Tertullian's allusion (*On Idolatry* 19) to the danger of idolatry that members of the officer class faced during this period. The issue of bloodshed does not come up at all here, and, in fact, Marinus' impending promotion indicates that his career as a soldier had not created problems of conscience up to that point.

A different situation obtains some thirty years later with

Maximilian, the first conscientious objector that we know about in the history of Christianity. In Numidia in the year 295 A.D. he was brought by his Christian father to the proconsul Dion in order to be enrolled officially in the service and to be measured for a uniform. During the proceedings the following exchange is recorded to have taken place:

> 1-2[34] Dion, the proconsul said, 'What is your name?' Maximilian answered, 'What do you want to know my name for? It is not right for me to serve in the army since I am a Christian.'
>
> Dion said, 'Get him ready.' While this was being done, Maximilian responded, 'I cannot serve in the army; I cannot engage in wrongdoing; I am a Christian.'
>
> Dion remarked, 'Measure him.' When this had been done, the staff member called out 'He is five feet, ten.'
>
> Dion said to the staff member, 'Give him the seal.' But Maximilian continued to resist saying 'I'm not going to do it; I cannot serve in the army.'
>
> Dion said, 'Join up if you don't want to die.' 'I will not,' Maximilian replied. 'Cut off my head. I will serve in the army of my God, not in any that belongs to this world.'
>
> Dion the proconsul said, 'Who has led you to this position?' 'Only my own soul,' replied Maximilian, 'and he who called me.'
>
> Dion said to the young man's father Victor, 'Talk to your son.' Victor replied, 'He knows what's at stake and can counsel himself about the best course of action.'

[34]Text: *Acts of the Christian Martyrs,* ed. Musurillo, OECT, 244.

To Maximilian, Dion the proconsul said, 'Join up and accept the military seal.'

'I will not take it,' he answered, 'I already have a seal, the seal of Christ, my God.' Dion said, 'I'll soon send you to your Christ.' 'If only you would!' he answered, 'That would be glory for me.'

Dion said to the staff member, 'Give him the seal.' Maximilian would have none of it, and he remarked, 'I am not going to receive a seal that belongs to this world. If you put it on me, I will smash it because it has no power. I am a Christian; I may not carry a piece of lead around my neck now that I have accepted the saving seal of my Lord Jesus Christ, son of the living God. You know nothing about him, but he suffered for our salvation, and he was delivered up by God for our sins. It is he whom all of us Christians serve; it is he whom we follow as life's sovereign and as the author of salvation.'

Dion said, 'Join up and receive the seal or you will die a miserable death.'

'I won't die,' Maximilian replied. 'My name is already in the presence of my Lord. I cannot serve in the army.'

Dion said, 'Consider your age and join up. It is fitting for a young man to do so.'

Maximilian answered, 'I am committed to serve my Lord; I cannot serve in an army of this world. As I have already said, I am a Christian.'

Dion the proconsul said, 'The sacred bodyguard of our sovereigns Diocletian and Maximian, Constantius and Maximus, includes Christian soldiers who serve.'

'They know what is in their own best interest,' Maximilian answered, 'but I am a Christian, and I cannot do what is wrong.'

Dion said, 'What are they doing that is wrong?''You know what they do,' Maximilian answered. Dion the proconsul said, 'Join up. Do not bring a miserable death upon yourself by disdaining the service.'

Maximilian answered, 'I am not going to die. And if I leave this world, my soul goes on living with Christ my Lord' (*The Acts of Maximilian* 1-2).

From this account it is clear that the young recruit's fundamental objection to serving in the army was religious, i.e. for him, as for Tertullian (*On the Crown* 11.1; *On Idolatry* 19.2), the seal of baptism and the seal of military service are incompatible. He cannot serve two masters. Maximilian's threat to break the lead seal bearing the emperor's image may suggest that there was an attendant problem of idolatry here, but nothing specific is said on that point. A division within the Christian community over the issue of military service is also evident because the magistrate notes that there were other Christians serving in the army even among the emperor's personal troops. Maximilian acknowledges that each man must follow his own conscience on the matter, but unfortunately he does not specify what evils he is talking about when he says to Dion, 'You know what they [i.e. Christian soldiers] do.' In reading this document one has the impression that the young man took exception to the whole character of military life and that it was this fact which made it impossible for him to serve. However exceptional his position may have been, there are indications (if we can believe all the details of the martyrdom) that he was held in high esteem by Christian contemporaries because we are told at the end of the narrative that he was buried in Carthage next to St. Cyprian.

Three years after this event at Tingis in North Africa we have another instance in which the military oath and the issue of idolatry again come into play. In 298 A.D. on a feast day honoring the emperors Diocletian and Maximilian a centurion named Marcellus threw down his military belt in the presence of fellow officers and proclaimed to them, "I serve in the army of the eternal king Jesus Christ, and from now on I cease to be a soldier of your emperors. And I disdain the worship of your gods made out of wood and stone because they are images that are deaf and dumb" (*The Acts of Marcellus* 1.1). When brought before the prefect of the legion to explain this violation of military discipline, Marcellus reiterates his position:

> 2.1[35] When you were celebrating your emperor's feast day on the 21 of July, I publicly announced in a loud voice and in the presence of this legion's standards that I was a Christian and that I could not honor a military oath made to him but only one made to Jesus Christ, the son of God, the almighty Father (*ibid*. 2.1).

Marcellus' trial was subsequently transferred to another jurisdiction, and when he was questioned once more, he replied, "I threw down my arms because it was inappropriate for a Christian serving in the army of Christ the Lord to do the same in the armies of this world" (*ibid*. 4.3). For this violation of military discipline he was sentenced to death. In this account there is no mention of bloodshed or other immoral acts associated with military life. Likewise there is nothing said about what other Christians in the army were or were not doing. From Marcellus' point of view it was simply a problem that the gulf separating Christianity from paganism was such that it was impossible for him to remain in the army. His superior saw his action as a case of insubordination and dealt with it according to the usual rules of military discipline.

The situation was a bit different for the veteran legionnaire Julius, who was martyred under Diocletian perhaps in the year 303 or 304 A.D. After the emperor had issued orders requiring all the troops in the army to sacrifice to pagan deities, Julius was brought before the prefect Maximus and charged with refusing to comply with this injunction. The dialogue which ensued between the prefect and the legionnaire is both revealing and touching.

[35]Text: *Acts*, ed. Musurillo, OECT, 250.

1.4[36] 'You know, do you not,' said the prefect, 'about the emperors' edicts enjoining you to sacrifice to the gods.'

'I know about them,' Julius replied, 'but I am a Christian, and I cannot do what you ask of me. I must not be unmindful of my living and true God.'

Maximus the prefect said, 'What harm is there in burning some incense and going about your business?'

Julius answered, 'I cannot show contempt for God's commandments and give the appearance of being disloyal to my God. Never in the twenty-seven years that I foolishly and mistakenly—so it seems—spent in military service was I called before a magistrate and charged either with a crime or with mischief-making. I have served in seven campaigns and never stood behind anybody or fought less bravely than anyone. My commanding officer never found fault with me. Do you think, then, that if I have been faithful in the past, I can be otherwise with commands of a higher order?'

'What is your military record?' asked the prefect Maximus.

'I served in the army,' replied Julius, 'and when my tour of duty was up, I re-enlisted. All the while I have worshipped in reverence the "God who made heaven and earth" (*Acts* 4.24), and even up to this moment I openly serve him.' The prefect Maximus said, 'Julius, I can see that you are a wise and responsible man. Take my advice. Offer sacrifice to the gods and receive a generous reward.'

Julius replied, 'I refuse to do what you ask in order to avoid eternal punishment.'

[36]Text: OECT, 260.

'If you consider it a sin,' replied the prefect Maximus, 'let me be at fault. I am the one who's exerting the pressure in order to avoid the appearance that you collaborated voluntarily. After it's over, you can go home without any fuss, collect your ten-year stipend and never be bothered by anyone again.'

Julius answered, 'Neither this money of Satan that you talk about nor your clever suggestion can rob me of eternal light. I cannot disown God. Pass sentence on me, then, as a Christian.'

'If you don't show some respect for the emperors' decrees and offer sacrifice,' said Maximus, 'I will have you beheaded.'

'That's a good idea,' replied Julius. 'I beseech you, my good prefect, by the prosperity of your rulers to carry out your design and pass sentence against me so that my prayers may be answered.' Maximus the prefect said, 'Unless you change your mind and offer sacrifice, you'll get your wish.'

'If I deserve to suffer in this way,' replied Julius, 'eternal glory is in store for me.'

'I'm giving you some advice,' Maximus said. 'If you were suffering for the sake of the civil laws, you would be held in perpetual honor.'

'I am certainly undergoing these sufferings for the sake of the laws,' answered Julius, 'but they are the laws of God.'

'You mean the laws,' said Maximus, 'that were passed on to you by someone who was crucified and is now dead? How silly it is for you to be more afraid of a man who is dead than you are of rulers who are alive.'

Julius answered, 'That man "died for our sins" (1 *Cor.* 15.3) in order to give us everlasting life. This

very same Christ is God who exists forever. Any
man who denies him will suffer eternal punishment.'

'Out of pity,' Maximus said, 'I am giving you some
advice. Sacrifice and go on living with us.' 'Living
with you,' Julius replied, 'will be death to me, but if I
die in the presence of God, I will live forever' (*The
Martyrdom of Julius the Veteran* 1.4-3.5).

Idolatry is quite clearly the issue in this account. There is
not a word about the evils of bloodshed or immoral behavior among the troops. One has the impression that in his
long career as a soldier Julius had never before found the
service at odds with his religious beliefs. He seems to have
been able to avoid participating in pagan rituals, but when
that kind of obligation was imposed upon him, there was no
room for compromise or subterfuge. The dilemma of the
prefect Maximus, on the other hand, and his sympathetic
efforts to accommodate Julius' conscience are evidence that
some pagans were reluctant to force the issue when the
question of military qualifications did not enter in.

These few documents help us to understand the disparate
problems which prevented some Christians, at least, from
enlisting or continuing to serve in the army. Idolatry,
bloodshed, oaths and the vices of military life all entered the
picture in determining a man's position on war and military
duty. The only general principle we can deduce from the
Acta is that no single issue was the source of the difficulty.
Circumstances and an individual's own sensitivity to the
precepts of the Gospels were the deciding factors, and a man
could expect to encounter varying degrees of approval or
criticism from his peers whatever choice he made.

This latter fact reflects the ambivalent attitudes toward
war and military service which seem to have been present in
the Christian community from the very beginning and
which became more pronounced as time moved on. Concomitant with the growth of explicit condemnation of
Christian participation in violence of any kind was a contin-
ual growth of Christians in the army during the first three
centuries. Whatever were the issues faced by Christian sol-

diers, increasing numbers of them were somehow finding it possible to remain in the service without compromising their faith, and this fact is a kind of unarticulated proof that the arguments of the pacifist writers were not universally persuasive.

There are hints in Tertullian that military service was being justified by appeals to both Old and New Testament texts, but beyond that we know little about the debate, if such there ever was, from the non-pacifists' viewpoint. What is notable in the period before Constantine is that both pacifist and non-pacifist positions existed side by side and that neither was able to supplant the other. That situation will not change in the fourth century. Even when the issue is "resolved" in non-pacifist terms, and ideas about the just war are developed, pacifist sentiments continue to be heard.

The reason for this is not far to seek because the fundamental issue raised by Tertullian, Origen and the early Lactantius did not go away. The feeling that bloodshed and killing are fundamentally opposed to love runs deep in the Christian conscience, and any claim that is made for the legitimacy of force has to be reconciled with this conviction. That task is not easy, and if the pacifist view was becoming increasingly inadequate for many Christians, it had not lost all its meaning. The acceptance by Christianity of war and violence as instruments of statecraft could not be a simple endorsement of governmental needs or desires, and, as we shall see, other problems now had to be faced which were heretofore unimagined.

PART II

THE POST-CONSTANTINIAN ERA

It is a truism that the reign of Constantine (306-337 A.D.) represents a watershed in the development of Christian attitudes concerning war and military service. The pacifist arguments of Tertullian, Origen and the early Lactantius now begin to subside, and the question is no longer whether participation in war is justified but what conditions should govern the right to declare war (*ius belli*) and what rules should be observed in waging it (*ius in bello*). For some critics this new outlook amounted to an abandonment of the pristine message of the Gospel and a relinquishing of the Christian ideal of peace. That would be true, I believe, if we were dealing with a thoroughly developed and generally uncontested position that was subsequently relinquished in order to accommodate temporal powers. From what we have seen, however, there was disagreement about the legitimacy of war and military service during the first three centuries, and some Christians were citing Scriptural texts in defense of a non-pacifist stance. These facts would indicate that the problem had not been settled, and we do well to speak of a development of Christian thinking in this area during the fourth century rather than of a volte-face on the issue.

One of the catalysts for this development was the very unexpected position in which Christians now found themselves vis-à-vis the Empire. The very thing which Tertullian considered impossible had, in fact, occurred. The emperor had become a Christian (in some of his attitudes and actions at least), and the earlier posture of abstention from participation in acts of violence and coercion appeared inadequate to the demands of the new situation. The notion, voiced but hardly developed by men like Melito and Tertullian, that Christianity and the empire were conjoint works of God intended to be mutually supportive now became a commonplace idea. Under these circumstances the problem that developed was that of defining the limits of these two works and of determining the precise ways in which they related to each other. Thus, it was imperative to clarify not only the role that secular power should play in spreading the new Faith but also the kind of individual and collective responsibility that Christians had for protecting and promoting the common good.

In trying to understand the attitude of Christians in the fourth century and in later ages, we should keep in mind that Constantine's rise to power and the concessions made to Christianity during his reign were unexpected boons that provoked an effusive, albeit sometimes uncritical, response. As one modern scholar has expressed it, "the need for loyalty to the State which accumulated in the Christians over three centuries, flooded the whole Empire like a high wave" (Aland, 125).[1] That wave brought problems of its own, but in the new atmosphere created by Constantine the feeling of being legitimate and of belonging to the political and social structure in ways heretofore impossible led Christians to adopt a new outlook. They obviously felt themselves less divided by their obligations to Church and state, and with the advent of a certain kind of peace they were undoubtedly less interested in forcing issues of potential disagreement. If they were in positions of authority, they must have been

[1]See p. 161.

impressed with the inescapable ambiguities involved in managing temporal affairs and thus less inclined to be apodictic in dealing with questions of public policy including that of war and military service.

In sum, it seems simplistic to speak of the Church's corrupting the evangelical principles of peace during the Constantinian era. A more accurate assessment would be that Christians were now wrestling with those principles in a new context and coming up with new answers. The whole process is perhaps one more illustration of the fact that the meaning of the New Testament is, to some degree at least, not the same for every age, and that it cannot be reduced to a single equation.

In the fourth century, as in any era, there were Christians who wished to simplify the problem in another way by identifying the interests of God's kingdom with those of earthly realms. In this scheme of things temporal wars are not seen as the result of sin or as a necessary evil but as the work of God himself exercising his will through fire and the sword. This vision, which easily leads to the concept of the holy war with all its blurring of secular and spiritual values, appealed to some, but the major thrust of Christian thinking followed other lines. As we shall see, the concept of the just war strikes a middle ground between the absolute rejection of violence as an instrument of statecraft and the sanctification of it as God's own instrument in managing the affairs of men. The path leading to that middle ground in the fourth century is not always straight or readily apparent, but its general direction is reasonably clear.

1. Eusebius of Caesarea (ca. 260-ca. 340 A.D.)

More than anyone else in the period following Constantine's accession, Eusebius, Bishop of Caesarea, reflects the intense spirit of loyalty that begins to make itself felt in the Christian community. With the cessation of persecution and the acceptance of Christianity as a legitimate religion,

Eusebius foresaw an easy and uncomplicated partnership developing between the Church and temporal rulers. Under such circumstances it was natural for him to lend whole-hearted support to the belief espoused earlier by writers like Tertullian, Clement and Origen, that the *pax Augusti* was part of God's plan in promoting the spread of the Gospel.

    3.7[2] When one realizes that Christ's disciples would have found travel to far-off places difficult if nations were at odds with one another and there were no contact among them because of all their different forms of government, who would not agree that it was through God's help that this (i.e. the solidifying of power under Augustus) coincided with the spread of the doctrine concerning our Savior. With the removal of such division, the disciples fulfilled their appointed task free of fear and intimidation after the God of All had paved the way for them and, through fear of a superior central authority, held in check the superstitious spirits of people in the cities everywhere. If errant polytheists were not restrained in any way from opposing the teaching of Christ, think how much internal strife you would find in city and countryside; how many persecutions and wars of no ordinary kind there would be if superstitious men had control of those areas. Holding in check the enemies of his own Word by fear of a superior central authority was also the work of the supreme God, for he wanted that Word to advance each day and to reach all men (*Demonstration of the Gospel* 3.7.140; cf. 8.3 and *Preparation for the Gospel* 1.4).

But this is not all. For Eusebius the centralizing of power in the hands of Augustus was more than a matter of clearing away obstacles to evangelization. The monarchy and the spread of the Gospel were, in fact, two blessings which came

[2]Text: GCS Eusebius, 6.146.

forth from God at the same time and which were intended from the start as integrated and integrating forces in the establishment of God's kingdom on earth. Together they brought to fulfillment the Old Testament prophecies concerning universal peace and harmony among men. In his panegyric of Constantine, which was delivered in 336 A.D., Eusebius makes this point in effusive terms.

16.3[3] One God was proclaimed to all the world; one Roman empire flourished everywhere, and the implacable and undying hatred that had always existed among enemy nations was completely swept away. As knowledge of the one God spread to all men and with it the saving teaching of Christ, which is the one path of true piety, at that very time a single ruler sprang up for the whole Roman empire, and a deep peace embraced the whole world. By the command, as it were, of the one God, two blessings sprouted forth simultaneously, that is, the Roman empire and the doctrine of true piety.... Concomitant with the proclamation of the One God and the one way of knowing him a single empire held sway among men, and the whole human race was converted to peace and friendship when all men recognized each other as brothers and discovered their natural kinship.... Thus, the pronouncements of the ancient oracles and the sayings of the prophets were fulfilled. Their statements are too numerous to set forth here, but included among them are the words proclaimed about the saving Logos: 'He will rule from sea to sea and from the rivers to the ends of the earth' (*Ps.* 72.8). And again, 'In his days righteousness and fullness of peace shall spring up' (*Ps.* 72.7). 'And they shall beat their swords into plowshares and their spears into pruning hooks. Nation shall not lift sword against nation, and they will no

[3]Text: GCS Eusebius 1.249.

longer learn the arts of war' (*Is.* 2.4) (*In Praise of Constantine* 16.3-7).

Whatever exaggerations there are in a rhetorical statement like this, the underlying assumptions are quite unmistakeable. If the apocalyptic vision of Rome as a devouring beast at war with God's saints is one extreme, what we have here is almost the opposite. Not only is the hand of God working simultaneously in the spiritual and temporal realms, but his purposes are clearly discernible at both levels. What is more, Eusebius' conviction on this matter is not confined to rulers of an earlier day. Constantine, no less than Augustus, is the recognizable agent of God in promoting the welfare of God's kingdom on earth. By following a long-established Greek tradition concerning the nature of kingship and by adopting a vision of history in which Constantine is the fulfillment of the promises made to Abraham, Eusebius gives us a view of the emperor that is quite new for a Christian writer in its intensity and explicitness.

> 2.3[4] As the common Savior of all men plays the part of the good shepherd faced with wild animals by using his invisible and divine power to keep at bay the rebellious spirits that flit about in the air and attack men's soul, so, too, the Savior's friend [i.e. Constantine], armed as he is against his foes with the standards given him by the Savior from above, subdues in battle and chastens the visible enemies of truth (*In Praise of Constantine* 2.3).

Through a type of imagery and parallelism familiar to pagan audiences, Eusebius here describes the close ties that bind religious and political affairs. Elsewhere he appeals to an Old Testament analogy to convey the significance of Constantine's famous victory over Maxentius at the Milvian Bridge in 312 A.D., a victory which consolidated the emperor's power and initiated a new stage in the history of the Church.

[4]Text: GCS 1.199.

9.9[5] Just as in the time of Moses himself and the ancient God-fearing race of Hebrews the chariots and army of Pharao, the pick of his horsemen, were hurled by God into the Red Sea and were drowned there and covered by the depths (*Exod.* 15.4-5), so, too, Maxentius 'plunged into the depths like a stone,' together with his soldiers and bodyguard as he was in the act of retreating before the divine power accompanying Constantine and was crossing the river in front of him. He himself had spanned this river quite effectively with pontoon boats and in doing so had wrought his own destruction. Thus, we might apply to him the words, 'He dug a pit, hollowed it out and fell into the hole he had made. His efforts shall come back on his own head and his wrongdoing shall fall upon himself' (*Ps.* 7.15-16). . . . [All this was done] so that those who had received a victory from God might fittingly emulate, in deed if not in word, the followers of the great servant Moses and sing the same hymns that were recited of old against the ungodly tyrant: 'Let us sing to the Lord. He has covered himself in glory; horse and rider he has cast into the sea. The Lord is my helper and protector; he is my salvation' (*Exod.* 15.1-2). And, 'Who is like You among the gods, O Lord? who is like you, magnified in holiness, marvelous in glorious deeds, worker of wonders? (*Exod.* 15.11) (*Ecclesiastical History* 9.9.5-8; cf. *Life of Constantine* 1.39).

Analogies like this in Eusebius are not just occasional flourishes generated by enthusiasm for the new political dispensation. In a persistent, if not always perceptive, vision of Constantine's reign the bishop sees the emperor as the vicegerent of God, doing his will and receiving blessings in return. Speaking of Constantine's conversion, Eusebius says,

---

[5]Text: GCS 2.2.828.

1.6[6] He accomplished this and publicized it like a good and faithful servant, openly proclaiming himself a slave and freely acknowledging that he was subject to the Ruler of All. God soon rewarded him by making him lord and master, the only victor among all those who had held power who was unconquered and unconquerable. God made him such a consistently triumphant ruler and glorious victor over his enemies that no one ever heard the like of him in human memory. Beloved by God and supremely blessed, he was so reverent and fortunate that he subdued with greatest ease more nations than any previous emperor, and he kept the realm intact up to the very end (*Life of Constantine* 1.6; cf. 1.46).

In a context like this, it is all but superfluous to raise the question of the *ius belli* in Eusebius' thought. For him the reality of Old Testament wars is not a problem but a precedent. God's ties with his servant Constantine are almost as close as they were with the heroes of the Old Testament, and the fact that Constantine prays to Christ "his ally" before entering battle (*Ecclesiastical History* 9.9.2) should be no cause for consternation. Indeed, it is fair to say that for Eusebius the justice of a particular war hinged on whether the conflict was initiated by the emperor or by somene else. In their war against Maxentius and Maximin both Constantine and Licinius are depicted as allies of the Almighty in liberating Rome from tyranny (*Ecclesiastical History* 9.9.1-2); later, when Licinius challenges Constantine for sole leadership in the Empire, he is portrayed as a man with "the depraved habits of the godless tyrants" and as a usurper who was waging "an impious and most frightful war" (*Ecclesiastical History* 10.8.2-3).

Given Eusebius' understanding of Constantine's role in the Divine plan, it is not surprising to find him extolling certain Christian aspects of the emperor's military campaigns. Not only is a Christian symbol (the labarum) placed

[6]Text: GCS 1.1.17

on the soldiers' standards and brought into play at difficult moments "as if it were a victory-producing charm" (*Life of Constantine* 2.7; 4.21), but Christian bishops are invited to join Constantine on the march because "he thought he ought to include in his retinue individuals who were necessary for divine worship" (*Life of Constantine* 4.56.2). If we have here what appears to be the first solid evidence for the existence of military chaplains, the reason cited by Eusebius for the bishops' acceptance of Constantine's invitation is very telling: they agreed to accompany him and "to fight together with him by means of their prayers to God" (4.56.3). What this suggests is that a new distinction is developing with regard to the Christians' role in defending the empire. For Origen, as we have seen, praying for the success and safety of the imperial armies was the most that any Christian was allowed to do. The injunction against bloodshed and killing applied equally to all the faithful. Eusebius implies that spiritual support in the form of prayer is appropriate for the clergy, but that the Christian soldier on the battle line is expected to do his part no less than his pagan colleague.

It is easy to see that this distinction between clergy and laity introduces a new element into the problem of reconciling the peaceful counsels of the Gospel with the requirements that the empire be defended against attack. What it suggests, in brief, is that for some Christians who are charged with particular responsibilities and who play a particular role in the Church, the principle of pacifism is absolute; for others with different responsibilities and a different role to play it is not. Ultimately this distinction rests on the principle of two states or levels of perfection within Christianity, a principle which is endorsed elsewhere by Eusebius in much broader terms.

> 1.8[7] As a result, two life styles have been established in   ˎ
> the Christian Church. The first, which goes beyond
> nature and the usual manner of life, is not involved

[7]Text: GCS 6.39.

at all with marriage, children, property, or an abundance of possessions. Out of an extraordinary love for things heavenly it departs from the common and customary pattern and is devoted wholly to the worship of God.... The other is subordinate and more concerned with human affairs. It is involved with chaste marriages, procreation, and the management of the home. It lays down practical rules for those fighting in a just war. While not forgetting its religious duties it gets involved in managing the fields, the market place and other affairs that have more to do with civic life. For men leading this kind of life special days are set aside to do penance, to study, and to hear the word of God. For such individuals there is a secondary state of perfection which is suitable in its own way for their kind of life. Thus, no one is excluded from sharing in the Savior's coming. Every race of men, Greek and barbarian alike, enjoys the benefit of the Gospel's teaching (*Demonstration of the Gospel* 1.8).

Whatever one thinks of this division of Christian responsibilities and however one assesses the attitudes toward war that were developing in Eusebius' time, it is at least clear that the terms of moral discourse on the topic are no longer what they were in the first three centuries. Both the growth of Christians in the army and the new feeling of cooperation that developed between temporal and ecclesiastical authorities made it difficult to endorse the simple solutions of the past. If it cannot be said that Eusebius himself thought very deeply about new approaches to the problem of Christian involvement in war, his comments do indicate that the dimensions of the issue had changed or had, at least, become more complex.

2. Official Church Documents and the Eastern Fathers

The complexities of the problem and some of the changes in the Church's public posture toward war and military service are reflected in official pronouncements that were issued in the fourth century. In 314 A.D., only two years after Constantine's victory at the Milvian Bridge, the Synod of Arles promulgated among its canons the following: "Those who throw down their arms in time of peace are to be separated from the community" (Canon 3). The exact wording of the Latin text of this canon has been the subject of much scholarly debate, but the principal point of contention is the meaning of the phrase "in time of peace." Are Christian soldiers being warned against desertion from the army during the periods in which no military compaigns are under way or during periods when there is no conflict between the Church and the state, i.e. when there is no persecution? In the first instance what the pronouncement says, according to some scholars, is that the Christian should serve in a peacetime army when the most he would be called upon to do is police work and when desertion from the ranks would cause unnecessary scandal to his pagan colleagues. In periods of combat, however, it is taken for granted that he will refuse to serve. According to this reading the canon maintains the pacifist stance found in the literary tradition while admitting the possibility that under certain conditions military service could be reconciled with Christian faith.

In favor of such a reading is a statement contained in a letter of Constantine which is recorded by Eusebius and which reads in part as follows:

> 2.33[8]   Those who previously served with honor in the military ranks but abandoned the service because of harsh and unjust circumstances, that is to say, because they valued the profession of their faith in

---

[8]Text: GCS 1.62.

God more than their own glory, should decide for themselves whether they are content to remain in the rank where they had been or to get out with an honorable discharge. It is right and appropriate for one who had demonstrated generosity and perseverance amid the kind of sufferings inflicted on these men to enjoy either retirement or service according to his own desire (*Life of Constantine* 2.33).

In all likelihood the "harsh and unjust circumstances" mentioned here refer to the persecutions under Diocletian and Galerius, and what Constantine is suggesting is that soldiers who had lost rank to avoid idolatry during such times could choose either to return to their former position or receive an honorable discharge. If one couples this statement with the Canon of Arles, it is easy to conclude that the Church responded to Constantine's act of generosity by issuing a decree designed to forestall any mass desertion from the army by Christian troops during times when they would not be called upon to engage in combat. In this way a compromise was effected which took cognizance both of the pacifist principle of the pre-Constantinian era and of the emperor's need for a standing army. Because this interpretation goes a long way in preserving continuity with the past, it has much to recommend it.

For the present writer, however, it remains unconvincing. I am not persuaded that the distinction between police work and military campaigns was ever a meaningful one for Christians in the early centuries of the Church.. The physical violence involved in both activities is indivisible, and the idea of Christians' serving during periods of relative calm but deserting when war threatened is simply not credible. No emperor, either Christian or pagan, could endorse or tolerate an arrangement of that kind. I suggest that what the Canon of Arles means is that when there is no persecution, i.e. when no threat of idolatry exists, a major hurdle to military service has been removed, and in such circumstances it was the duty of the Christians, as well as non-

Christians, to support the empire even by serving in combat when necessary. This reading of the text runs counter to much of the literary evidence of the first three centuries, and in terms of that tradition it represents a departure from tradition. On the other hand, in terms of the growing practice among Christians during the third and fourth centuries it represents a confirmation of what was actually taking place, and it suggests that an effort was being made by Church authorities to deal with existing realities and with the demands placed on Christians by their new position in the empire.

In 325 A.D., however, the Council of Nicea issued a decree which appears to undercut that of Arles. The text of Canon 12 reads in part as follows:

> 12[9] Those who responded to the call of grace and initially expressed their faith by putting off the military belt, but who subsequently acted like dogs returning to their vomit when they offered money and gifts in order to get back into the army must remain among the hearers for three years and then among the supplicants for ten more.

Although this statement would appear to mark a return to the strict pacifist principles of the first three centuries, it is, in fact, not as stringent or universal as would first appear. The context indicates that it was not military service itself but service in the army of Valerius Licinius, Constantine's rival, that was being forbidden. Since Licinius had abandoned Christianity and was engaged in persecuting the Church, the danger of idolatry and apostasy in the army was revived during his reign, and it was this threat that the Council was warning against. Thus, Canon 12 applies to a very specific case, and it would have broader implications only if recruitment or reenlistment involved circumstances similar to those that obtained in the time of Licinius, i.e. only if service in the army meant compromising one's faith through idolatry.

[9]Text: C.J. Hepele, *A History of the Christian Councils*, 1.417.

Some ten or fifteen years after this Canon we get further evidence that changes were occurring in the Church's official views on war and military service. In the so-called *Canons of Hippolytus,* a late fourth or early fifth century compilation of disciplinary and liturgical rules from earlier periods, we read the following:

XIV.74[10] A Christian should not voluntarily become a soldier unless compelled to by someone in authority. He should have a sword, but he should not be commanded to shed blood. If it is ascertained that he has done so, he should stay away from the mysteries at least until he has been purified through tears and lamentation. He should fulfill his obligation without deceit and in fear of God (Canon XIV).

In the development of Christian thinking on war and military service this particular canon, which is dated between 336-340 A.D., is significant on several counts. It reiterates the principle that Christians should stay out of the army, but at the same time it acknowledges that it is not always possible to do so. Furthermore, it recognizes that Christian soldiers will at times be forced to take human life. If both of these possibilities are decried, provisions are, nonetheless, made for dealing with cases in which the ideal was not realized. Quite obviously, instances of the latter kind were becoming sufficiently widespread to warrant a more flexible pastoral approach to the problem. By requiring penance of those involved in bloodshed instead of excluding them completely from the community, the Canon indicates that circumstances had changed and the older intransigence regarding military service was no longer workable. This is a first step toward a reevaluation of the issue as a whole.

A somewhat similar approach is taken by the Cappadocian writer St. Basil (ca. 329-79 A.D.), who distinguishes between war and murder but nonetheless has reservations about the propriety of killing.

[10]Text: TU 6.4.82.

188.13[11] Our predecessors did not consider killing in war as murder but, as I understand it, made allowances for those who fought on the side of moderation and piety. Nonetheless, it is good to admonish those whose hands are unclean to abstain just from communion for three years (*Letter* 188.13).

If not all forms of bloodshed are at odds with Christian beliefs, Basil cannot divest himself of a certain sense of incongruity between the two. He thinks that all those who have engaged in violence should not have intimate contact with sacred things without first undergoing a form of purification. As we shall see, it was this kind of sensitivity that led his contemporary St. Ambrose to insist that his clergy refrain altogether from the use of physical force.

Though Basil is aware of the vainglory that often accompanies armed conflict (*Homily on Psalm 61*.4), he does not hesitate to argue that the military profession is compatible not only with Christian faith but on rare occasions even with sanctity. In a letter written to a soldier whom he had met on an earlier occasion and whose company he recalls with deep satisfaction, he says,

106[12] I have become acquainted with a man who demonstrates that it is possible even in the military profession to maintain perfect love for God and that a Christian ought to be characterized not by the clothes he wears but by the disposition of his soul (*Letter* 106).

In light of this experience it is not at all untoward to find Basil citing military figures from the New Testament as models of Christian life. In a homily on the soldier-martyr Gordius, he depicts the saint as following in the footsteps of the centurion at the cross (*Matthew* 27.54), the centurion at Capernaum (*Matthew* 8.8-10) and Cornelius in *Acts* 10 (*Homily* 18.7). The latter two are, of course, traditional

---

[11]Text: PG 32.681.
[12]Text: PG 32.513.

exempla cited during the first three centuries by non-pacifists to justify Christian participation in the army.

The gradual shift in Christian views on war and military service that was taking place at this time is reflected obliquely in a remark of St. Athanasius (ca. 296-373 A.D.) in one of his letters (*To Amun*) written before 356 A.D. Speaking about the role which circumstances play in establishing the morality of an action, he says,

> [13] One is not supposed to kill, but killing the enemy in battle is both lawful and praiseworthy. For this reason individuals who have distinguished themselves in war are considered worthy of great honors, and monuments are put up to celebrate their accomplishments. Thus, at one particular time, and under one set of circumstances, an act is not permitted, but when the time and conditions are right, it is both allowed and condoned.

Athanasius' point is merely a brief observation in a much larger discussion, and it includes no specific reference to Christianity at all. Nonetheless, it is this kind of distinction between murder and warfare that now comes to the fore, and the issue no longer is whether Christians may take human life but what conditions are necessary to justify such action. That kind of shift marks a significant departure from the concerns of the ante-Nicene period, and, as we shall see, it lies at the center of the ideas set forth by St. Ambrose and St. Augustine on justifiable war.

Before turning to these writers, however, we shoud note the different approaches taken by eastern and western Christian writers of the fourth century A.D. on the issue of war and military service. For the most part eastern writers were preoccupied with peace within the individual soul and peace within the Christian community. As one modern scholar has described the situation in relation to the Cappadocian fathers, "they placed the interests of religion

[13]Text: PG 26.1173.

at the heart of their philosophy, caring only to safeguard its unity and solidarity, which was so severely threatened. Their reactions were less strong when conflict between two peoples or a civil war broke out. They then felt themselves men of party, involved in the outcome of a struggle, and could not assess the problem serenely and impartially" (Zampaglione, 274). Though it is difficult to deal with the issue of war and violence "serenely and impartially" in any context, what is significant is that the whole problem of public and private responsibility in this area and the moral limits surrounding the *ius belli* and the *ius in bello* were never serious topics of interest in the minds of the eastern writers. Indeed, the manner in which St. John Chrysostom (ca. 347-407 A.D.) and, in the next century, Cyril of Alexandria (d. 444 B.C.) interpret the *pax Romana* as the fulfillment of Isaiah's prophecy reflects a naiveté about contemporary events that makes such issues irrelevant to their concerns.

In the west, however, we have a different situation. Here the lines separating imperial and ecclesial responsibility were always more clearly drawn, and the rivalry between temporal and spiritual powers was a persistent trait. In such a context the rules that should govern Christian behavior in the public arena were spelled out more concretely, and one is not surprised to find men like Ambrose and Augustine dealing with war and military service in rather specific terms. This is not to suggest that western writers were any less inclined than their eastern colleagues to find the ultimate sources of war in the divided heart, but they tended to be more aware of the ways in which these factors were played out in the area of power and politics. On that score the western fathers made a unique contribution to subsequent speculation on war during the Middle Ages and in later times.

3. St Ambrose of Milan (ca. 339-397 A.D.)

It is apparent from what we have seen thus far that a shift in Christian thinking about war and military service was taking place in the course of the fourth century. Despite the ambiguities and unsolved problems which the decline of pacifist sentiment entailed, it was obvious that principles of non-violence would neither dominate in the Roman political structure nor bring about an abandonment of force as an instrument of statecraft. If Christian ideals of peace, forgiveness and forbearance were going to have any role to play in the public sphere, they would have to be integrated into the larger question of justice and order in society, and they would have to operate in a world that was neither free from sin nor secure against violent threats from many quarters. In such a context Eusebius' unsophisticated endorsement of imperial power and authority was as simplistic an answer to the problem as Tertullian's pacifism was. What was needed at this juncture was some recognition of the concrete issues involved when Christians had responsibility for living up to the Gospel while at the same time they were directly accountable for for managing the affairs of state. Specifically, what had to be faced was the problem of maintaining the principles of Christian love when the demands of statecraft called for the use of force. Only when writers came to grips with this issue could there be any hope of striking a middle ground between uncritical acceptance of war and violence and a total relinquishing of statecraft by responsible Christians.

The two writers who sparked reflection on this point in the fourth century and who were most influential in determining the limits of the problem for later ages were St. Ambrose and St. Augustine. Although the latter's writings on war and violence are more extensive and better known than Ambrose's, the Bishop of Milan anticipated Augustine in several important respects, and he must be considered a major figure in the development of Christian thinking on war. While examining his views, one must keep in mind that Ambrose's election as bishop in 374 A.D. occurred while he was enjoying a distinguished public career and was, in fact, governor of the province of Aemilia-Liguria in Northern Italy. It should come as no surprise, then, that his attitudes on war and violence were much influenced by Roman sentiments of justice, loyalty, courage and public responsibility.

Ambrose says quite plainly that "the kind of courage which is involved in defending the empire against barbarians, or protecting the weak on the home front or allies against plunderers is wholly just" (*On the Duties of the Clergy* 1.27.129). He talks of courage in war as noble and comely "because it prefers death to slavery and disgrace" (*Duties* 1.41.201), and he speaks with pride about the fearlessness of Old Testament figures such as Joshua, Jonathan and Judas Maccabeus (1.40.195). If a man fighting for personal gain deserves condemnation, that same individual is in quite a different position when he risks his life for the welfare of his country.

> 3.3[14] There is nothing that goes against nature as much as doing violence to another person for the sake of one's own advantage. Natural feeling argues that we ought to look out for everyone else, to lighten the other man's burdens and to expend our efforts on his behalf. Any man wins a glorious reputation for himself if he strives for universal peace at personal risk to himself. Everyone believes it is much more commendable to protect one's country from destruction than to protect oneself from danger and that exerting oneself for one's country is much superior to leading a peaceful life of leisure with all the pleasures it involves (*Duties* 3.3.23).

Because Ambrose shares the typical Roman abhorrence for civil war, he does not hesitate to condemn such conflicts (*Apology for the Prophet David,* 1.6.27), and in his eulogy of the Emperor Theodosius he describes the dead usurpers, Maximus and Eugenius, as souls in Hell "teaching by their wretched example how dreadful it is to take up arms against one's rulers" (*On the Death of Theodosius,* 39). Wars against barbarians and others who do not share the faith, however, are a different matter. Since such people are natu-

---

[14]Text: PL 16.151.

ral enemies they are a legitimate object of attack as well as a legitimate target for usury. In his treatise *On Tobias* where he deals with the latter issue, Ambrose talks about the law of the Old Testament regarding usury and gives his own interpretation.

15.51[15] Consider the text of the Law: 'You will not exact interest from your brothers; you will exact it from a foreigner' (*Deuteronomy* 23.19-20). At that time who was a foreigner if not Amalech, Ammoreaus or other such enemies? From such people the Law says, 'Exact interest.' That is to say, you can legitimately demand interest from someone whom you have every right to wish harm to and against whom you can lawfully wage war....Demand interest from him whom it is no crime to kill. The man who demands interest fights without a weapon; he who exacts interest of an enemy, avenges himself without raising the sword. Thus, usury is legitimate where-ever war is legitimate. 'Your brother,' in this context is, first of all, everyone who shares the faith and, secondly, every Roman....(*On Tobias* 15.51).

Although the simplistic division of friends and enemies on the basis of national and/or religious affiliation does reflect certain typical sentiments of Ambrose, we should be cautious about pressing the point too hard. As we shall see, he did not endorse the killing of unorthodox believers, and it seems that he learned a lesson from the one instance in which he thought he saw the hand of God assisting the imperial armies against barbarian heretics.

Despite his concern for preserving orthodoxy and maintaining the security of the empire, Ambrose insists on the need to distinguish between just and unjust wars (*On Duties* 1.176), and in specifying the conditions that should govern both the *ius belli* and the *ius in bello* he follows traditional Roman principles. Thus, a war that is designed to punish

[15]Text: CSEL 32.2.547.

wrongdoing (*Duties* 3.19.110; 116) or is defensive in nature (*Duties* 1.35.176-77; 1.27.129) is justified, as is one undertaken to gain possession of territory that has been promised by God (*Duties* 3.8.54). In the latter case we are dealing, of course, with Old Testament wars, and Ambrose takes it for granted that such conflicts are clear evidence that not all wars are immoral. With respect to the *ius in bello* the bishop makes it clear that agreements with the enemy should be kept (2.7.33), that no unfair advantage should be taken of him ("if a time or place for doing battle with the enemy is agreed upon, it is considered unjust to anticipate one's opponent on this score since it makes a difference whether a man is defeated in combat or through some advantage or happenstance [*Duties* 1.29.139]), and that mercy should be accorded a foe in defeat (*Duties* 3.14.87; *Discourse on Luke's Gospel* 5.76).

It would be simplistic and misleading, however, to suggest that Ambrose is merely putting the stamp of Christian approval on common Roman practices and principles while paying little attention to the evangelical precepts about peace and forbearance. He is aware that the "whole purpose of virtue and physical courage is to re-establish peace when war is over" and that "military courage itself very often militates against peace" (*Discourse on Psalm 118,* 21.17). He states unequivocally that "it is not permissible for a Christian to withhold his love even from his enemies" (*ibid.* 12.51), and he is sensitive to the different approaches that are called for by the Old and the New Law in this regard:

> 5.73[16] The law calls for reciprocal vengeance; the Gospel commands us to return love for hostility, good will for hatred, prayers for curses. It enjoins us to give help to those who persecute us, to exercise patience toward those who are hungry and to give thanks for a favor rendered (*Discourse on Luke's Gospel* 5.73).

For Ambrose one of the most obvious instances in which this advice is to be followed quite literally is in the matter of

[16]Text: CSEL a32.4.210.

personal self-defense. On this point the Bishop of Milan, in his *Duties of the Clergy* is a pacifist.

3.4.27[17] Some people inquire whether a wise man caught in a shipwreck can or should take a life preserver away from a fool. Though common opinion would argue that it is better to have the wise man escape drowning than the fool, it does not seem to me that a Christian who is both wise and just should try to save his own life at the expense of another's. Indeed, even if a man comes up against an armed thief, he cannot return blow for blow lest in the act of protecting himself he weaken the virtue of love. The Gospel supports this position in a clear and obvious way: 'Put up your sword; everyone who kills with the sword will be killed by it' (*Matt.* 26.52). Who is more detestable than the thief, the persecutor who approached Christ with an eye to bringing about his death. But Christ who sought to cure everyone through his own wounds did not want to be protected by doing harm to his persecutors (*Duties* 3.4.27).

Violent self-defense is unacceptable in Ambrose's view because it inevitably destroys the virtue of love—elsewhere called piety—which unites man to God and is the foundation of all the other virtues (cf. *Discourse on Psalm 118*, 18.45; *Discourse on Psalm 36*.37). Harming an assailant in order to protect one's own life or property is tantamount to preferring a human good to a divine one, and such a reversal of the proper hierarchy of values undercuts any benefit that might accrue from preserving one's life.

The same principle does not apply, however, whenever a third party is involved. Here Ambrose is very explicit.

1.36.178[18] The glory that courage brings resides not only in strength of arm and body but in the virtue of the

---

[17]Text: PL 16.152.
[18]Text: PL 16.75.

soul, and the essence of the virtue is not to be found in inflicting injury but in preventing it. For anyone who does not prevent an injury to a companion, if he can do so, is as much at fault as he who inflicts it. Following this principle Holy Moses provided an early proof of his courage. For when he saw a Jew being injured by an Egyptian, he defended his countryman to the point of killing the Egyptian and hiding him in the sand (*Duties* 1.36.178).

The significance of this statement for the development of Christian ideas on violence and war is difficult to exaggerate. What is denied to an individual in his own case is not only permitted but morally required of him when it comes to defending another against aggression. Moreover, the example cited by Ambrose makes it evident that he is not thinking of passive resistance alone. The responsibility for looking out for one's neighbor can require a person to use force on another's behalf even to the point of taking an aggressor's life. In such circumstances love and extreme violence are not mutually exclusive; in fact, the implication is that love demands the use of force. For all subsequent discussion of the problem of war in a Christian context this is a critical point, and, as we shall see, it plays a very important role in Augustine's thinking about the legitimacy of using force.

The distinction which Ambrose makes here between self-defense and defense of another tells us little about the precise way in which the use of force can be reconciled in an individual's conscience with the Gospel precepts about loving enemies and turning the other cheek. Although it cannot be said that Ambrose ever adequately dealt with this issue, there is some indication in his writing that he was aware of the problem and that he tried to cope with it in a limited way. The relevant text is a long passage in his *Discourse on Psalm* 118 (15.15-22) where he attempts to understand David's words in verse 113 ("I have hated the evil and have loved your law") in light of the Gospel precepts on love. David's restraint in dealing with Saul and Absalom is indication enough for Ambrose that the verse as a whole should not be read literally. He then goes on to suggest two other possibilities. First, that the term "hatred" really amounts to "preference," and that it indicates the need to put limits on human attachments so as to avoid letting them get in the way of love for God. On the other hand, the word may be read literally, and in that case it must refer, says Ambrose, to evil deeds rather than to evil men.

15.22[19]   Therefore, it was not evildoers but evil words that David hated, for when he said, 'I have hated evil' he did not add the word 'man.' Given the fact that Christ says in the Gospel, 'Love your enemies' (*Matt.* 5.44) and the Apostle says, 'Bless those who persecute you, and do not curse them' (*Rom.* 12.4), what excuse will a man living according to the principles of the Gospel have for hating wrongdoers? You should interpret the words as meaning that he hated evil itself rather than evildoers, who, despite their actions, are subject to conversion through the preaching of the gospel (15.22).

In short, the hatred mentioned here must be directed at the wrong rather than the wrongdoer, who is always susceptible to a change of heart. Thus, violent acts of the kind which David's life was filled with need not destroy one's love for others.

The importance of this rather banal distinction between person and act should not be underestimated. What Ambrose's remarks here demonstrate is that the issue of violence and war is a personal as well as a public issue. For Ambrose no less than for Origen or Tertullian the fundamental problem is how an individual can maintain within himself a spirit of love while in the very act of using force. If the bishop's answer to this question is ultimately open to debate, he at least shares the concern of the Ante-Nicene writers for the issue. If, in fact, he abandoned the pacifist practices that they felt were inexorably tied to the law of love, he tried hard not to abandon the law itself.

[19]Text: CSEL 62.5.341

To a large degree Ambrose was a public man, and much of what he had to say on war and violence was part of his whole approach to the rights and responsibilities of temporal rulers. In some respects he resembles Eusebius in his confidence about the hand of God working on both the temporal and spiritual levels. Thus, he shares the view held by the Bishop of Caesarea and others before him that the peace of Augustus was designed by God to prepare the way for the Gospel.

21[20] To be sure, before the expansion of the Roman Empire, not only did kings of individual realms fight against one another but the Romans themselves were being worn down with civil conflicts. . . . . As a result of all this, weariness with civil war led to the empire's being put in the hands of Julius Augustus, and in this way internal struggles were brought to an end. Thus, Augustus made it possible for the apostles to be sent immediately throughout the world at the command of the Lord Jesus, 'Go and teach all nations' (*Matt.* 28.19). They gained access even to those realms which had been closed to them because of disturbances among the barbarians. Thomas visited India and Matthew Persia. To enable the apostles to visit more parts of the earth Augustus expanded the power of the Roman empire everywhere in the world at the very time when the Church was getting started, and he brought together in peace people of different outlooks and territories that were far distant from one another. He taught all men to live under one temporal power and to acknowledge in their expression of faith the rule of the one omnipotent God (*Discourse on Ps. 45.*21).

What is more, in his own day Ambrose thought he detected the hand of God working through the imperial armies. In 378 A.D. as Gratian was setting out to assist his uncle

[20]Text: CSEL 64.343.

Valens against the Goths, who were Arian Christians, the bishop offered encouragement by predicting that a prophecy of Ezekiel was about to be fulfilled. In a treatise titled *On the Faith*, which was hastily put together for the emperor's benefit, Ambrose was carried away by the analogy between Gog and Goth, and he addressed his sovereign in almost apocalyptic terms:

2.16.136[21] I ought not to detain you with many words, O Emperor, intent as you are on war and preoccupied with victory over the barbarian. Go forth, then, protected by the 'shield of faith' and holding the 'sword of the spirit.' Go forth to the victory promised in days past and foretold by the Scriptures. For in those days Ezekiel prophesied the devastation we have suffered and the wars with the Goths. We read in the text, 'Prophesy, therefore, Son of Man, and say, "O Gog, the Lord says this: 'When my people Israel is living in peace, is it not true that you will rise up and come from your dwelling place in the far north, and many nations will come with you, a great and powerful mass of mounted troops. And you will come to my people Israel to cover the earth like clouds in the last days, etc.' " ' The Gog he speaks of is the Goth, whom we now see on the move, and it is the approaching victory over them that is promised us in the words of the Lord: 'And they will take booty from those who have done the same thing to them; they will despoil those who took spoils from them, says the Lord. On that day I will give to Gog,'—that is to the Goths,—'a famous spot in Israel for a grave, a gathering place of countless men who came to the sea. And the encircling valley will cover Gog and bury him with all his hosts, and it will be called the Land of Gog's Horde. The house of Israel will bury them in order to purge the land in seven months' (*Ezekiel* 39.10-12). Almighty God,

with your own blood and devastation we have paid
enough and more than enough for the death of the
faithful, the exile of priests and the horror of such
great impiety. It is abundantly clear that those who
have abandoned the faith cannot remain
untouched. Turn, O Lord, and raise the banners of
faith. . . . Show us now a clear sign of your majesty
so that with the help of that majesty he who believes
that you are the true 'power and wisdom of God' (I
Cor. 1.24), not temporal or created but, as it is
written, the 'eternal power and divinity of God' (cf.
Rom. 1.20), may win trophies of his faith (*On the
Faith* 2.16.136-43).

The disastrous defeat of the Roman army at Hadrianople
which occurred before Gratian arrived with his troops was a
total reversal of Ambrose's expectations, and he undoubtedly came to regret this misplaced enthusiasm of his early
episcopacy. At least we never hear talk of this kind in his
subsequent writings. But if history proved Ambrose wrong,
his initial self-assurance on this occasion is indicative of the
kind of thinking the new political dispensation in the empire
could provoke. That particular mind-set was to become all
too prevalent in subsequent centuries, and, as might be
expected, it created problems that are not easily solved.

Ambrose's involvement in other areas of public concern
reveals both strengths and weaknesses in his handling of the
problem of violence and coercion. The bishop showed himself a product of his own day when he endorsed legislative
measures (including fines and confiscation of property)
against heretics and non-believers. At the same time, however, he rejected the death penalty as means of effecting
religious conformity, and he would have nothing to do with
the Spanish bishops who had executed the heretical Priscil-
lian (*Letter* 24.12 and 26.3). His position on this matter is
summed up by a comment in one of his letters where he is at
pains to distinguish the wrong from the wrong doer. "When
a guilty man is put to death, it is the individual rather than
the sin that is punished; when the guilt is laid aside, forgiving

the individual is equivalent to punishing the sin" (*Letter* 26.20).

On the other hand, when rioting Christians burned the synagogue at Callinicum in 388 A.D., and Theodosius prescribed that the expense of rebuilding it should be borne by the local bishop who had instigated the uprising, Ambrose's reaction was anything but supportive. In a long letter addressed to Theodosius he warned the latter against handing the Jews a victory over the Church and scandalizing the faithful by rebuilding a "house of impiety, a shelter of madness under the condemnation of God himself" (*Letter* 40.14). The bishop's actions here leave the impression that violence against non-believers is a matter of no consequence, and if it can be argued that he was at least partly motivated by fears of further bloodshed, it is obvious that his sense of justice was crippled by religious bias.

Nonetheless, Ambrose did not shrink from challenging the emperor himself when he thought that the latter had used force unjustly. In 390 A.D. Theodosius massacred some 7,000 people at Thessalonica in order to punish the city for murdering the Roman commandant there. For this crime Ambrose excommunicated the emperor until he did public penance. Thus, if the bishop conceded that it was legitimate for public authorities to have recourse to the use of force, he also insisted that there were definite limits to that right.

The dilemma which sensitive Christians faced when they were charged with the responsibility for maintaining a reasonable level of order and justice in society is laid out in Ambrose's response to a Roman magistrate who had problems of conscience about imposing the death penalty in criminal cases. When asked for advice on the matter, Ambrose replies that he would hesitate to give a reply to this controversial issue were it not for Paul's words in *Romans* 13.4 about the purpose of the judge's "sword." Thus, if it is to the credit of some magistrates that they abstain from imposing the death penalty, those who refuse to follow this course should not be condemned. But there is more to be said:

25.3[22]   You see, then, what power your authority gives you
and what tack mercy leans towards. You are justified if you exercise your right, and you will be
praised if you do not. If you cannot bring yourself
either to exercise it or punish wrongdoers in a squal-
id prison, but you free them, you will win greater
approval from me in my role as a priest. After the
case is heard, a guilty man could receive the kind of
sentence that would allow him subsequently to
plead for mercy or at least to remain in prison
'without grave suffering,' as someone has expressed
it. I know that many pagans are in the habit of
glorying over the fact that they have returned from
their provincial governorships without bloodying
the executioner's axe. If this is the tack which those
men take, what do you suppose Christians should
do (*Letter* 25.3).

In short, mercy is the better course because there is always
hope for the wrongdoer's conversion. However legitimate
capital punishment might be, for Ambrose it remains in
some sense out of step with what is essentially Christian.

It is for this reason, no doubt, that he forbids his clergy
any participation in acts of violence or physical coercion.
"Interest in matters of war seems to be foreign to our role,"
he tells his priests, "because we are concerned with matters
of the soul rather than of the body, and our activity has to do
not with weapons but with peaceful deeds" (*On Duties*
1.35.175). Here we have an explicit statement of what was
implied earlier in Eusebius' remark about the role of the
bishops who accompanied Constantine's army. The responsibilities of laity and clergy are distinct, and the latter should
have no direct involvement in the use of arms. Elsewhere, in
more general terms, Ambrose makes the same point about
the Church as an institution.

8.49[23]   The church, however, does not conquer the forces
opposed to it with temporal arms but with the arms

[22]Text: PL 16.1040.
[23]Text: PL 16.249.

of the spirit, which are capable in the sight of God of destroying the fortresses and heights of spiritual wickedness (cf. II *Cor.* 10.4)....The Church's weaponry is faith; the Church's weaponry is prayer, which overcomes the adversary (*On Widows* 8.49).

Ambrose followed his own principles in this regard when in 385 A.D. he had a serious confrontation with the imperial court over the transferring of a Catholic basilica to the Arians. He offered only passive resistance to the emperor's troops who threatened him and his congregation, and he stated his position very succinctly when he said: "I cannot hand over the basilica, but I must not fight" (*Letter* 20.22).

In dealing with some of the moral problems faced by Christians who endorse the use of force, Ambrose cannot escape a more fundamental conflict that is part of human nature. That is, man's struggle with his own passions (*Discourse on Psalm 118,* 20.46). Although what he has to say on this theme has both pagan and Christian precedents, it bears mentioning here because of its relationship to external conflicts and because it is an integral part of all Christian discussion on violence, especially that of St. Augustine. Ultimately for Ambrose the struggle for peace is waged not with barbarians, heretics or other nations but within the individual soul. Unless the battle is won there, there will be no end to external conflicts.

5.58[24.] Unless you first free yourself from all stain of sin so as to prevent your interior disposition from giving rise to dissension and strife, you cannot provide a remedy for others. In the area of peace begin with yourself so that when you have established peace there, you can take it to others. For how can you purify the heart of others unless you have done the same to yourself first (*Discourse on Luke* 5.58).

And elsewhere he says,

[24]Text: CSEL 32.4.204.

> 2.6[25] The peace which removes the enticements of the passions and calms the perturbations of the spirit is loftier than that which puts down the invasion of barbarians. For it is a greater thing to resist the enemy inside you than the one far off (*On Jacob* 2.6.29).

The kind of peace Ambrose is talking about here will come only as a divine gift at the close of time (*Discourse on Psalm 36*.22); in the meantime one must acknowledge that man's struggle with the forces within him is sometimes successful, sometimes not. It is this latter fact, as we shall see, which preoccupies much of Augustine's thinking on war and violence and which puts a definite stamp on his own views of the matter.

4. St. Augustine of Hippo (354-430 A.D.)

No writer of the early Church has contributed more to the development of Christian attitudes regarding war, violence and military service than St. Augustine. As the one who is commonly credited with being the author of the "theory of the just war" and as the only theologian in the early centuries of Christianity to endorse and to discuss openly the use of coercion for suppressing religious dissent, he occupies a critical position in the history of the problem. In order to understand his ideas on these issues, however, we need to keep several points in mind.

The first is that Augustine never composed a specific treatise on Christian rights and responsibilities regarding war. His remarks on the subject are scattered through a great variety of works including sermons, commentaries, letters and apologetic pieces, which were written over a period of more than thirty years and which were concerned, for the most part, with other issues. This fact inevitably affected the kind of problems he chose to discuss and the

[25]Text: CSEL 32.2.49.

way in which he handled them. For example, in the treatise *Against Faustus* his defense of Moses' use of force must be viewed in the context of his whole approach to the Old Testament and his preoccupation with maintaining an essential unity between the Creator God and the God of the New Testament.

Again, his assurances to the Roman general Boniface that military service is quite compatible with Christian faith are part of a deep concern over the havoc and destruction caused by the Vandal invasions in the early part of the fifth century. All of which is not to suggest that Augustine tailored his views to suit the occasion but that there is little in his writing on war which springs from theoretical musings or from a dispassionate examination of the question. Augustine's comments in this area are regularly designed to respond to a particular issue, and his statements are not always easy to reconcile. If he is clear and coherent on certain dimensions of the problem, he treats other aspects of it in a cursory way or ignores them altogether. Nowhere do we find in his works anything that could be called a "theory of the just war," and we are on safer grounds if we speak about his attitudes and his approach to the issue rather than his "doctrine" of the just war.

Augustine's ideas on war, violence and military service hinge on a few basic assumptions concerning man's present condition in the created world and the role of the state in human society. On both of these issues it is hard to overemphasize the importance of Original Sin in the bishop's thinking. As a consequence of Adam's fall the human race became a "mass of sin" (*To Simplicianus on Diverse Questions* 1.2.16), which was fundamentally at odds with God and merited his condemnation (*City of God* 21.12). Even with the advent of salvation in Christ man's tendency to follow his own selfish interests and lower appetites remains all but irresistible, and this fact threatens the very structure of human society. Under such conditions (summed up in Augustine's famous phrase *libido dominandi,* the lust for domination), God wills the civil order as means of punishing wrongdoers and restraining evil.

153.6[26] Surely it is not in vain that we have such institutions
as the power of the king, the death penalty of the
judge, the hooks of the executioner, the weapons of
the soldier, the stringency of the overlord and even
the strictness of a good father. All these things have
their own method, reason, motive and benefit.
When they are feared, evil men are held in check,
and the good enjoy greater peace among the wicked
(*Letter* 153.6.16).

If Augustine was inclined to reject Eusebius' notion that
Rome was God's agent in abetting the spread of Christianity, he was far from rejecting temporal power in any apocalyptic sense. He is fond of citing Paul's words in *Romans* 13
on the role of civil rulers in society, and he insists that
disobedience to properly constituted authority is disobedience to God himself (*Against the Letters of Petilianus*,
2.20.45). "Obedience to rulers is a general stipulation of
human society," he says in his *Confessions* (3.8.15), and the
danger of unraveling the social and political fabric through
insubordination and rebellion always loomed very large in
his mind.

In a symbolic description of the human condition that has
become a classic in western literature Augustine argued that
all men may be classified either as citizens of the City of God
(i.e. believers following the word of God) or as citizens of the
earthly city (lovers of self). The inhabitants of the two
"cities" are divided from one another by the objects of their
love as well as by their goals, habits and ultimate destiny.
However, since the two "cities" are intermingled with one
another in the world of time, and the inhabitants are not
easily distinguishable, the welfare of the City of God is
inextricably bound up with that of the earthly city. If a well
constructed or well-ordered temporal government cannot
provide the kind of justice (*vera iustitia*) that will ultimately
prevail in God's kingdom, it does contribute to the mainte-
nance of some measure of equity on this earth (*City of God*,

[26]Text: CSEL 44.413.

19.17), and it does provide that modicum of peace or "tranquility of order" (*City of God* 19.13) which is essential to the continuance of any society. If Christians ultimately think of themselves as aliens passing through the earthly city, they should, nonetheless, value the "peace of Babylon," as Augustine calls it, (*City of God* 19.26) no less than their pagan associates do.

This notion of peace and its importance to all men is an integral part of Augustine's views on temporal power, and for a man who is credited with putting the Christian stamp of approval on war and violence it is remarkable how often he returns to this point.

15.4. . .[27] It is wrong to say, however, that the things which this earthly city desires are not good since, in fact, the city in its own human way is better off with them. To achieve a minimal kind of benefit it desires an earthly peace and strives to obtain this through war. If it is victorious and its opponents disappear, there will come a peace which the warring parties did not possess when they fought with one another in their sad state of need over things which both of them could not have. This is the kind of peace which 'glorious victory,' as they call it, brings. When victory goes to those who have fought in the more upright cause, who would doubt that such a victory should be celebrated. Who would doubt the resulting peace is desireable. These are blessings, and are unquestionably gifts from God. But if we overlook the higher goods which are part of the heavenly city where victory will be secure in a peace that is everlasting and supreme, and if those other goods are desired in such a way that they are thought to be the only ones, or are valued more than those which we believe to be superior, then misery will surely follow, and what misery was there already will surely increase (*City of God* 15.4).

[27]Text: CCL 48.457.

Difficulties arise when earthly peace and the blessings of this world are mistaken for the ultimate good that is attainable only in the Heavenly City. Barring that confusion, however, the Christian no less than other men should be grateful for the limited peace that is attainable in a sinful world.

In a way, he cannot help doing so because in Augustine's mind the quest for peace is something which lies at the heart of every man and every society whatever be their immediate goals or their way of life.

19.12[28]   Anyone who takes even a superficial look at human affairs and at the nature we all share recognizes with me that everybody desires peace just as everyone wa.its joy. Even those who opt for war want nothing else but victory; thus their aim is a glorious peace through war. For what is victory but the conquering of opponents, and once that occurs, there will be peace. Even those whose aim is to test their military skill by exercising command, or engaging in combat fight wars for the sake of peace. Thus, it is clear that peace is the desired end in war. In the very act of fighting every man is pursuing peace; nobody, on the other hand, makes peace in order to have war (*City of God* 19.12).

This last statement forms the core of Augustine's advice to the Roman general Boniface in a letter written in 418 A.D. giving the bishop's ideas about how a Christian soldier should conduct himself.

189[29]   Peace should be your aim; war should be a matter of necessity so that God might free you from necessity and preserve you in peace. One does not pursue peace in order to wage war; he wages war to achieve peace. And so, even in the act of waging war be careful to maintain a peaceful disposition so that by defeating your foes you can bring them the benefits

[28]Text: CCL 48.675.
[29]Text: CSEL 57.135.

of peace. 'Blessed are the peacemakers,' says the Lord, 'for they will be called the sons of God' (*Mt.* 5.9). If peace is such a delightful dimension of man's temporal happiness, how much sweeter is the divine peace that belongs to the eternal happiness of angels. And so, let it be because of necessity rather than your own desire that you kill the enemy fighting against you (*Letter* 189.6).

And whatever glories accrue to the man who fights on behalf of his country in a just cause—glories which Augustine himself, as we shall see, was quick to acknowledge—the peacemaker who wields the word instead of the sword is following a higher call. Writing to Darius, an ambassador who had been sent to North Africa in the winter of 428-29 A.D. to negotiate a settlement between the imperial court and a revolutionary faction led by Boniface, Augustine makes this point very clearly.

229.2[30] Preventing war through persuasion and seeking or attaining peace through peaceful means rather than through war are more glorious things than slaying men with the sword. If those who engage in combat are good men, they are undoubtedly striving for peace, but they do so by shedding blood; your charge, however, was to prevent bloodshed. That is your good fortune in contrast to the others who are required to kill (*Letter* 229.2).

Augustine's sensitivity to the need for peace was based, in part at least, on his own experience with the horrors of armed conflict. Having lived through the period of Alaric's sack of Rome in 410 A.D. and seeing the spread of the Vandal armies across North Africa toward the end of his life, he had reason to decry the sufferings of war and the wretched state of man that leads inevitably to bloodshed. Justified or unjustified, war is an evil that only those who have lost their humanity can experience without sorrow.

[30]Text: CSEL 57.498.

19.7[31]   They tell us, however, that the wise man will wage just wars. As if the wise man, when he recalls his own human limitations, will not all the more decry the fact that he was forced to do so. For, unless the wars were just, he would not have to wage them, and in such circumstances he would not be involved in war at all. It is the other side's wrongdoing that compels the wise man to wage just wars, and even if that wrongdoing gave rise to no unavoidable conflicts, it should cause man sorrow because man is responsible for it. Let everyone grieve when he thinks about the truly shocking and cruel evils involved here, and let him acknowledge his miserable state. Any one who endures these things or thinks about them without sorrow in his heart is all the more unfortunate in considering himself happy because, in fact, he no longer possesses any human sensitivity (*City of God* 19.7).

In all Augustine's comments on war and peace these words are, perhaps, his most succinct statement of the problem. Both the "wrongdoing of the other side" and the necessity that compels the wise man to take up arms are a result of sin. If Augustine acknowledges a real difference between just and unjust wars, the ultimate truth of the matter is that in an imperfect world the just man, no less than the scoundrel, is faced with imperfect choices and with the harsh realities that flow from them. Though he would have it otherwise, he is often forced to choose among evils, and in doing so he can be called fortunate only in a relative sense.

4.15[32]   Waging war and expanding the empire by conquering other peoples strikes evil men as a fortunate thing, but to good men it is simply a necessity. Since, however, it would be worse for good men to be under the thumb of wrongdoers, it is not out of line to describe such a necessity as 'fortunate' (*City of God* 4.15).

[31]Text: CCL 48.672.
[32]Text: CCL 47.111.

It is along these same lines that Augustine justifies a Christian's serving as a judge in the criminal courts even though such a position entails acts of violence that are objectively wrong. In Book XIX of the *City of God* where, among other things, he discusses the problems of human society, he reviews some of the limitations under which all judges operate and sums up by asking,

19.6[33]   Amidst all these dark corners of public life in society will the wise man sit as judge or not? Undoubtedly he will. For society, which he considers it truly immoral to cut himself off from, constrains him and forces him to fulfill this obligation. He does not consider it a sin that innocent witnesses are subjected to torture in someone else's trial, or that the accused who are tortured despite their innocence frequently give in to the pain and, after making false confessions, are punished in spite of their innocence; or that they often expire under torture or as a result of it even without being condemned to death; or that the accusers themselves are condemned by a judge who does not know the facts when the charges they bring—perhaps from a desire to serve society and to punish crime—are true but cannot be substantiated in the face of false witnesses and a defendant who fiercely resists torture and makes no confession. All these horrible things the wise judge does not consider sins inasmuch as he does them not out of desire to do harm but because of unavoidable ignorance and a judgment that he cannot shirk because society requires it of him. This is the kind of misery in the human condition that I am talking about even though no evil intent is involved. If the wise man's inescapable ignorance and the necessity of passing judgment forces him to torture and punish innocent men, is it not enough that he be considered guiltless without needing to be happy as well? On the con-

[33]Text: CCL 48.670.

trary, how much more sensitive and more in tune with his humanity is it for him to recognize the misery involved in that necessity, to loathe it in himself, and, if he is reverent and wise, to cry to God, 'Deliver me from my necessities' (*Psalm* 25.17) (*City of God* 19.6).

Such "necessities", however, do not gainsay the fact that wars are often provoked by the lust for power and renown. In the early books of the *City of God*, where Augustine's polemic against Rome's wars of conquest is most virulent, he leaves little doubt about his feelings on this score. He is particularly incensed by the spirit of vanity which makes of battle a glorious affair.

3.14[34]   This lust to dominate inflicts great evils on the human race and wears it down. Overwhelmed by it Rome exulted in her victory over Alba and used the term glory to describe the accolades she received for her crime because, as our Scriptures say, 'in the desire of his heart the sinner wins praise and the wrongdoer is commended ' (*Psalm* 10.3) Tear away the false and misleading disguise so that we may see the facts as they are. Let no one say to me, 'This man or that one is great because he fought with so and so and beat him.' Gladiators, too, are victorious. Their kind of cruelty also wins praise as its reward, but I think it is better to suffer the consequences of any kind of lethargy than to seek glory in that kind of fighting (*City of God* 3.14).

Even with the spread of Rome's dominion and the concomitant decline in foreign conquests there was no end to wars sparked by such motives.

19.7[35]   Although there has not been, nor is there now, a dearth of foreign enemies against whom we have always waged war and do so to this very day, none-

---

[34]Text: CCL 47.77.
[35]Text: CCL 48.671.

theless, the extent of the empire itself has generated wars of a worse kind. I am talking about social and civil wars which shake the human race in even more miserable fashion either when they are actually going on as a means of achieving peace or when fears of a new outbreak are present. If I wanted to do justice in my comments to the many different disasters, as well as the harsh and dire necessities bound up with these evils, there would be no end to my remarks, and still I could not hope to treat them adequately (*City of God* 19.7).

Thus, whatever be the blessings of peace and whatever sufferings are involved in foreign and domestic conflicts, neither history nor man's moral predicament offers hope for a world free of war. "Over the course of the centuries," Augustine asks in one of his letters (199.10.35) "have we ever had a time when the world was not scourged by war in one place or another?" And in the *City of God* he provides an answer to his own rhetorical question.

17.13[36]   In the great ebb and flow of human affairs no people has ever been granted such security that it did not have to fear attacks on its life here below. The place that has been promised for that kind of peace and security is an eternal one. It is set aside for eternal souls in Jerusalem, the free mother, where the people of Israel in the true sense of the word will dwell, for the word Irael means "seeing God" (17.13).

Augustine's pessimism concerning man's fallen state and the wars which inevitably flow from it is matched by an overriding conviction about two things: that ultimately in God's providence everything works to the good and that God uses war both to chastise the wicked and to test the faithful. Whatever be the human motives or justifications for war, God works his will in this area in ways hidden to man. It is this conviction which lies behind Augustine's

[36]Text: CCL 48.578.

treatment of Old Testament wars in his treatise *Against Faustus.* The bishop's Manichaean opponent had contended that a violent and vindictive Jahweh who commanded Moses to slay his enemies was at odds with the spirit of Jesus and was completely foreign to the Christian vision of reality. In another context (*Questions on the Heptateuch* 6.10) Augustine countered such assumptions with a short statement that a war enjoined by God "is undoubtedly just, for there is no evil in Him." In replying to Faustus, however, he attempts to clarify what is at work in God's injunction to Moses.

22.74[37] He [i.e. Faustus] ought not to be surprised or horrified at the wars waged by Moses because even in that case Moses was following God's instructions and in doing so was acting out of obedience rather than a spirit of savagery. Nor was God's action in ordering such wars inhuman. He was inflicting just punishments and striking terror in the hearts of those who deserved it. What is it about war, after all, that is blameworthy?. Is it that people who will someday die anyway are killed in order that the victors might live in peace? That kind of objection is appropriate to a timid man, not a religious one. What rightly deserves censure in war is the desire to do harm, cruel vengeance, a disposition that remains unappeased and implacable, a savage spirit of rebellion, a lust for domination and other such things. The reason why good men in the face of violent resistance even undertake wars at God's command, or the command of legitimate authority, is to inflict just punishment on things like these. That is to say, when they find themselves in that kind of situation in human affairs, right order constrains them to initiate such wars or to follow the commands of others in this regard (*Against Faustus* 22.74).

[37]Text: CSEL 25.672.

This statement is fundamental to an understanding of Augustine's approach to the whole problem of violence and coercion. If Israelite wars enjoined by God are incontrovertible evidence that not all wars, even in a Christian context, are immoral, that is true because Augustine reads the Old Testament differently from Origen or Tertullian. For him, there is no allegorizing of the text nor any attempt to see the Old Testament as an early stage in salvation history which is now superseded by the Christian dispensation. Actually Augustine hears two voices throughout the Scriptures: the voice of correction and the voice of mercy. They operate in tandem with now one and now the other calling man to action. For Augustine there are evils connected with war which are worse than death, and it is to correct these that men are allowed and sometimes required to take up arms. Thus, war, as one modern commentator has expressed it, is both "a consequence of sin and a remedy for it" (Russell, 16). And if God "regularly uses wars as a way of chastising and punishing sinful individuals and of testing through afflictions like this men who lead a just and praiseworthy life" (*City of God* 1.1), it is ultimately he who determines "the start, the progress, and the end of wars" (*ibid.* 7.30; cf. 5.22), and it is he who "decides the issue of who will be subjected in war and who will do the subjecting" (*ibid.* 18.2). Even when victory falls to evil men, we must see in this fact God's judgment "humbling the defeated by correcting or punishing their sins" (*ibid.* 19.15; cf. *Against Faustus* 22.75).

Neither Augustine's confidence in the ultimate workings of Providence nor his belief that particular individuals function as God's agents in rectifying wrongs removes the danger that acts of coercion will be governed by a spirit of cruelty and vindictiveness. For this reason he insists that such attitudes have no role to play in the use of force, and the analogy which he employs again and again to make this point is that of a father chastising his son.

138.2[38] These precepts about patience that we have been discussing must always be observed with respect to one's interior disposition, and a spirit of benevolence must always permeate the will so as to avoid returning evil for evil. On the other hand, we must do a lot of things with those who resist but who must be corrected with a certain kind of benign severity. We must look out for their welfare rather than cater to their own desires, a policy which their [i.e. the pagans'] literature praises very highly in a leader of state. For however harsh a father is in correcting his son he does not stop loving his offspring. The correction takes place, nonetheless, even though the young man resists and suffers from it because, willing or not, he seems to need a painful cure, a fact which the father would prefer to be otherwise and which is a source of grief to him. By analogy, if the earthly city observes Christian principles, even its wars will be waged with the benevolent purpose that better provision might be made for the defeated to live harmoniously together in justice and godliness. Anyone whose freedom to do evil is curtailed is subject to a beneficial kind of restraint since nothing is less fortunate than the good fortune of sinners. This latter promotes a kind of criminal impunity and enables an evil disposition to gain strength like an enemy in one's midst.... If it were possible, even wars would be waged as an act of mercy by good men so that by controlling unbridled passions they could stamp out those vices that ought to be removed or suppressed by any responsible government (*Letter* 138.2.14; cf. *Letter* 173.2).

However persuasive or unpersuasive the analogy of paternal correction may be, this statement indicates how far

[38]Text: CSEL 44.139.

Christian thinking—at least in the mind of its greatest Western theologian of the early centuries—had come from the pacifist mood of the Ante-Nicene writers. For the latter the notion of Christians waging war with a "benevolent purpose" was simply out of court, and if "benign severity" may not have been wholly foreign to their way of thinking, the suggestion that it could operate on an international level with Christian participation surely was.

It is hard, then, to overestimate the impact that Augustine had in arguing, as Ambrose did before him, that violence and an internal spirit of love are not mutually exclusive. "It is not military duty (*militia*)," he says in one of his sermons (302.15), "but malice of heart (*malitia*) that forestalls the doing of good." This principle is at the heart of his defense of justified war, and it is a point that he sees amply illustrated in both the Old and the New Testament. Moses' violence against the Israelites who had worshipped the golden calf (*Exodus* 32.25-29) is one obvious example, as Augustine points out in his reply to Faustus.

22.79[39] What, then, was cruel about Moses' commands or his actions when with a holy zeal and a desire that the people entrusted to him be subject to the one true God he saw that they had stooped to building and worshipping an idol and had defiled themselves with demons? What was cruel about his punishing them by summarily killing a few of their number with the sword, men whom God's own secret and hidden judgment had marked out for death because he had been offended by them? In this way he provided a salutary warning for the people of that time and established a precedent for handling such matters in the future. When one reads Moses' prayer for the sinful Israelites, who would not conclude that he did what he did out of deep love rather than any cruelty. 'If you are will-

[39]Text: CSEL 25.680.

ing to forgive them their sin, forgive them. Otherwise blot me from your book' (*Exod.* 32.32). Anyone who compares with sensitivity and reverence the execution [of the Israelites] and the prayer [of Moses] sees this point very clearly. When he observes a man loving so deeply and raging so violently, he sees how harmful to the soul it is to commit fornication through idols (*Against Faustus* 22.79).

Here, as so often in Augustine, the enormity of sin and the need for corrective action is the primary consideration, and this concern reappears when the bishop wrestles with New Testament texts that seem to exclude the use of force. More than once he argues that Christ's admonition about turning the other cheek pertains to the heart where "virtue has its dwelling" (*Against Faustus* 22.76) rather than to external actions, and he reiterates the dangers of allowing sin to go unchecked. In *On the Lord's Sermon*, he writes:

1.20.63[40] This text [i.e. about turning the other cheek] does not forbid punishment which serves as a corrective. In fact, that kind of punishment is a form of mercy. Nor does it exclude the principle of an individual's being prepared to endure greater sufferings at the hands of the one who is the object of correction. The only person suitable for inflicting punishment is the man whose love has driven out that normal hatred which rages in us when we have a desire for revenge. We do not have to fear, for instance, that parents seem to hate their young son if he has done wrong, and they box his ears to prevent a recurrence.... There are two things, then, that we ought to look for: first, that the one punishing has been given the authority to do so by the natural order of things, and, second, that he inflict punishment with the same kind of feelings

[40]Text: CCL 35.72.

that a father has toward his son who is still young enough that he cannot possibly be an object of hatred. This example is the best illustration of the fact that one can love and punish a son all at the same time rather than just letting him go undisciplined. The purpose, of course, is not to make the wrongdoer miserable through punishment but to bring him happiness through correction. On the other hand, the person doing the correcting is calmly prepared, if need be, to endure greater sufferings at the hands of him who is being corrected regardless of whether or not he has the actual power to coerce him.

Many holy men who are well aware that the separation of soul and body in death is not to be feared have, nonetheless, played on men's anxieties in this regard by inflicting capital punishment for certain sins. They do so in order to instill a salutary fear in the living and to protect those who are undergoing capital punishment from the harm they might suffer not at death's hands but through increased sinning which might continue if their life went on. Those whom God had given the power to make such a judgment did not exercise it rashly. Elias, for example, by his own hand and by fire called down from God slew a large number of individuals, and a good many other great and holy men, inspired by the same spirit of concern for human affairs, followed the same tack (*On the Lord's Sermon* 1.20.63-64).

Christ's injunction about not resisting evil, he says elsewhere (*Letter* 47.5), was intended, "to forestall our taking the kind of delight in revenge which feeds on another's misfortune; it was not meant to encourage us to neglect the correction of others." And in a letter to Boniface Augustine reiterates this interpretation of *Matthew* 5.39, arguing that Christ himself did not literally follow his own injunction about turning the other cheek.

138.13⁴¹ Accordingly, those commands pertain more to the interior disposition of the heart than to external actions, the idea being that we should maintain an interior spirit of patience and benevolence but do what seems most beneficial for those whose welfare we are bound to look out for. This point is evident from the reply made by Christ the Lord himself, a singular example of patience, when he was struck in the face. "If I have said something wrong, then point it out. If not, why do you strike me?" (*John* 18.23). Thus, he did not follow his own command if we take that command literally because he did not turn the other cheek to his assailant but told him not to compound the injury. Nonetheless, Christ had come prepared not only to be struck in the face but to die by crucifixion for those who inflicted these sufferings on him. It was for them that he prayed while hanging on the cross, "Father, forgive them because they do not realize what they are doing" (Luke 23.34). (*Letter* 138.13; cf. *On the Lord's Sermon* 1.19.57-58).

In giving practical advice to Boniface and in rejecting Manichaean pacifism Augustine appeals to examples from both the Old and the New Testament. Thus, Moses and David, as well as the centurion at Capernaum (*Mt.* 8.5-13), Cornelius in the *Acts of the Apostles* (chap. 10), and the soldiers who came to John the Baptist (*Luke* 3.14), all take on an importance which they did not possess in the mind of a pacifist writer like Tertullian. To Boniface Augustine says,

189.4⁴² Do not believe that it is impossible for anyone to serve God while on active duty in the army. Holy David, whom God was most pleased with, was a military man, and so were a good many just men

---

⁴¹Text: CSEL 44.138.
⁴²Text: CSEL 57.133.

of his time. The same is true of the centurion who said to the Lord, 'I am not worthy that you come under my roof, but only say the word and my child shall be healed. . . . ' The same is true of Cornelius to whom the angel sent by God said, 'Cornelius, your acts of charity have found acceptance and your prayers have been answered. . . . ' And then we have the men who came for baptism to John, the holy precursor of the Lord and friend of the Promised One, a man of whom the Lord himself remarked, 'Among the children born of women there is no greater than John the Baptist.' When these men asked John what they should do, he replied, 'Do not strike anyone or make false accusations. Be content with your pay.' If he told them to be content with their pay, he certainly was not telling them that they could not be soldiers (*Letter* 189.4; cf. *Letter* 138.15).

In *Against Faustus* Augustine repeats this argument about John the Baptist, reinforces it with a distinction between homicide and public duty and ties it in with Christ's advice about rendering to Caesar what is Caesar's.

22.77[43] If this (i.e. that war is sometimes necessary and justified) were not true, when the soldiers came to John for baptism and asked 'What are we to do,' he would have replied, 'Throw down your arms; leave the service. Do not strike, wound, or kill anyone.' But recognizing that when they do such things as part of their military duty they are not guilty of homicide but are administering the law, that they are not avenging private wrongs but protecting the safety of the state, he replied, 'Do not strike anyone; do not make false accusations. Be content with your pay.' (*Luke* 3.14). But since the Manichaeans are in the habit of openly reviling

[43]Text: CSEL 25.672.

John, let them listen to the Lord Jesus Christ himself commanding us to render to Caesar these very
funds which John says the soldiers should be content with. 'Render to Caesar what is Caesar's,' he
said, 'and to God what is God's (*Matt.* 22.21).
Providing salaries to soldiers who are required for
war is one of the things taxes are paid for (*Against
Faustus* 22.74).

The compatibility between Christian love and violence
in Augustine's scheme of things, and his insistence that
corrective action was called for in the face of wrongdoing,
did not gainsay the distinction between legitimate and
illegitimate use of force or between just and unjust wars.
In Augustine's mind such a distinction applies to every act
of violence, and it falls to human wisdom to determine
what criteria should govern both the *ius belli* and the *ius
in bello*. By drawing attention to such principles Augustine not only made significant contributions to the development of Christian thinking regarding the use of force,
but he also established the ground rules for discussion of
the issue in subsequent centuries.

Among the principles governing justifiable violence the
first has to do with authority. Only those who are
enjoined directly by God or who occupy positions of leadership in the state have the right to take human life. In
such circumstances an individual's responsibility for
promoting the common welfare is precisely what distinguishes him from a murderer. As Augustine makes clear
in his dialogue *On Free Will* (1.4.9.25), neither the soldier
killing the enemy nor the magistrate punishing the criminal is guilty of sin, and the bishop expounds on this point
in the opening book of the *City of God* where he attempts
to explain why all killing is not murder.

1.21[44]   The divine law we have been talking about made
certain exceptions to the principle that one may

---

[44]Text: CCL 47.23.

not kill a human being. Included in this category are individuals whom God by means of some law or an explicit command, limited to a particular time and person, has ordered put to death. Anyone who acts as a delegate in this regard is not himself the slayer since he is like a sword that is a tool in the hands of its user. Accordingly, men who have waged war at God's command or who have put criminals to death in their capacity as agents of the state in accordance with its laws, that is to say, on very justifiable grounds, have not violated the commandment, 'Thou shalt not kill.' . . . Except, then, in cases where there is some specific command from God, who is the source itself of justice, or where some just law that is generally applied demands it, any man who takes his own life or that of someone else is guilty of a homicide (*City of God* 1.21; cf. *Against Faustus* 22.70).

The principle that killing is justified only when sanctioned or ordered by legitimate authority applies to wars among nations as well.

22.75[45] It makes a difference for what reasons and under whose authority men undertake wars that are to be waged. The natural order of things, which is designed for the peace of mankind, requires that the authority for waging war, and the planning of it, rest with the chief of state. Soldiers, in turn, for the sake of the peace and safety of all are obliged to carry out a war that has been decided on (*Against Faustus* 22.75).

Making the head of state the sole authority for determining the justice of a particular war entails obvious difficulties both because the ruler is not a neutral party in arriving at such a decision and because it is difficult in

[45]Text: CSEL 25.673.

such circumstances to speak of collective moral responsibility vis-a-vis any conflict. We must remember, however, that Augustine was living under a highly centralized and authoritative form of government, and that without some criterion of this kind he could foresee no way of limiting wars on the national and international level. For their part the soldiers in such a conflict are expected to obey their superiors. Far from being guilty of wrongdoing in taking human life, they are only doing what they must and should do by virtue of their position.

1.26[46]   If a soldier kills a man in obedience to his lawful superior, no civil law charges him with homicide; in fact, if he does not kill the individual, he is charged with dereliction of duty and insubordination. If, on the other hand, he had done the same thing on his own volition and authority, he would have committed a crime of homicide. Thus, he is punished for doing something on his own which he would be punished for neglecting to do under orders (*City of God* 1.26).

When we discuss the *ius in bello*, we will see whether the individual soldier has any freedom (and concomitant obligations) to use his own discretion in carrying out the commands of a superior, but it is clear, at least, that his position is different from that of a private citizen. In the latter's case Augustine, no less than Ambrose, appears to be a strict pacifist. He does not allow the use of force even in self-defense.

47.5[47]   I do not approve of killing another man in order to avoid being killed oneself unless one happens to be a soldier or public official and thus acting not on his own behalf but for the sake of others, or for the city in which he lives. Provided, of course, that one possesses legitimate authority and acts in accordance with his position (*Letter* 47.5).

[46]Text: CCL 47.27.
[47]Text: CSEL 34.2.135.

We have seen that Ambrose criticized self-defense on the grounds that it inevitably involves a violation of the love which is owed to every man. For Augustine the evil of self-defense lies in the fact that it entails an inordinate desire (*libido*) for the goods of this world including temporal life itself.

This point is discussed at length by the bishop and his pupil Evodius in Book I of the dialogue *On Free Will* where the topic under discussion is the role that passion plays in wrongdoing. After it is agreed by the bishop and his interlocutor that blameworthy desire (*libido*) may be defined as "the love of things which can be taken away from a man despite his own will," i.e. the love of things which are ultimately outside man's control, Augustine asks whether killing an attacker in order to protect one's own life, freedom or virtue necessarily involves inordinate desire. Evodius replies,

1.5.11[48]   How can I suppose that no inordinate desire is involved in the case of men who take up the sword to protect things which they can lose even against their will. Or, if they do have control over these things, what need is there for going to such lengths as killing a man for them?

Augustine:

Is the law unjust, then, which gives a traveler the right to slay a robber in order to avoid being killed by him? or which gives any man or woman the right, if he can, to slay a potential rapist before he makes his violent attack? The law goes so far as to command a soldier to kill the enemy, and if he refuses, his commander punishes him. We will not venture, will we, to claim that these laws are unjust or, more accurately, no laws at all since it seems to me that an unjust law is not really a law.

[48]Text: CCL 29.29.217.

Evodius:

I think the law is adequately protected against a charge like that because, in states where it is in force, it allows some latitude for doing lesser wrongs in order to forestall greater ones. After all, the death of a man plotting against somebody's life is a lesser evil by far than the death of one who is acting in self-defense. It is a much more monstrous thing for an innocent victim to suffer criminal attack than for the attacker to be slain by his potential victim. As for the soldier, he is the law's agent when he kills an enemy, and on this account it is easy for him to carry out his responsibility without getting embroiled in any inordinate desire. A law that has been enacted to protect the populace cannot be subject to a charge of passion. If indeed the man who enacted the law, did so at God's command, that is to say, at the command of eternal justice, his action could be free of the slightest tinge of passion. But even if he enacted the law under the influence of that vice, it does not follow that obedience to such a law necessarily involves any inordinate desire because a good law can be enacted even by an evil lawgiver.... No inordinate desire, then, need be involved in obeying a law which enjoins the use of counterforce against an enemy in order to protect the citizenry. And the same principle can be applied to all public servants who are subject to public authority by virtue of the law and the established order of things.

Nonetheless, if the law is blameless, I cannot see how those people we mentioned earlier can be without guilt since the law does not force them to kill but merely leaves the matter to their discretion. They are free to refuse to kill anyone for the sake of things which they can lose against their will and which on that account they should not be in love with in the first place. There may be a question in some people's minds whether the soul can be somehow destroyed when the body dies. If so, it is not worth much; if not, then there is nothing to be afraid of. As for chastity, who could have any doubt that its very existence depends on the soul since it is a virtue, and for this reason even the violence of a rapist cannot destroy it. In short, whatever the violent assailant who is slain was going to take from us is not completely in our control, and for this reason I do not understand how it can be called our own. Thus, while not blaming the law for allowing such assailants to be killed, I cannot find any way of justifying those who take such action.

Augustine:

For my part I am even less able to see why you should be looking for a way to justify anyone who is not guilty before the law.

Evodius:

Not guilty before the law, perhaps, but only with respect to laws which men can see and read. I am not certain that they are not guilty in the eyes of a more stringent and very hidden law, if nothing in the world actually escapes the hand of God's providence. In the eyes of that law how can they be free of sin if they pollute themselves with human blood in order to safeguard things that ought to be disdained. It seems to me, then, that the law which is written for governing a people justifiably permits such actions and that Divine Providence punishes them. The law governing a people employs such punishments as are adequate for maintaining peace among unsophisticated men and only to the extent that such punishments can be regulated by men. Offences against the law of

> God have their own kind of punishment from which, it seems to me, only wisdom can set man free.

Augustine:

> I praise and commend you for this distinction. Although it is only a start and not yet worked out, it is both bold and probing. In your view the law which is established for governing states allows a good deal of freedom and leaves many things unsanctioned which are, nonetheless, punished by Divine Providence. I think you are right, and we ought not to take exception to what a law does simply because it leaves some things undone (1.5.11.32-13.41).

The fundamental issue here is that an assailant can take from his victim only those things (including life itself) which the latter will inevitably relinquish at some time in the future and over which he has no ultimate control. The one good which is at risk, i.e. one's virtue, is, in fact, not the assailant's to take. Thus, killing another human being to protect temporal goods is an expression of inordinate desire and as such is culpable before God even if not punishable before the law. It is precisely because the soldier or magistrate acts on behalf of others that he is free of such desire and is thus allowed or even obligated under certain conditions to take another's life.

Proper authority, however, is not the only factor to be considered in determining the *ius belli*. Equally significant for Augustine are the motivations and/or provocations which generate armed conflicts. In this area the bishop is very clear about one point, namely, that wars of conquest or territorial expansion are immoral. "What else can we call it but larceny on a grand scale," he says early in the *City of God* (4.6), "when a nation wages war on its neighbors and then solely out of a desire for dominion moves on to grind down and suppress other nations that have done no harm." On the other hand, wars initiated to punish wrongdoing by another nation are justifiable. "As a rule just wars are defined as those which avenge injuries, if some nation or state against whom one is waging war has neglected to punish a wrong committed by its citizens, or to return something that was wrongfully taken" (*Questions on the Heptateuch* 6.10).

Several things should be noted in this latter statement. First, Augustine is speaking of offensive rather than defensive wars, and it is clear that the recovery of lost property is a legitimate reason for taking up arms. Here we have a striking contrast to the restrictions placed on an individual with respect to preserving temporal possessions. Obviously, too, war is considered a means not only of restoring a situation to the *status quo ante* but of punishing wrongdoers as well, and this is in line with what we have seen earlier in the bishop's thought about the use of coercion as a remedy for sin. Also, in light of what we have seen, is it not surprising that Augustine finds a classic instance of justifiable aggression in the Old Testament. He argues that in refusing the Israelites free passage through their territory the Amorites violated a nation's natural rights, and this was reason enough to warrant the use of force.

4.44[49]   One ought to note how just wars were waged. Harmless passage, a right which ought to have been granted according to the most reasonable standards governing human society, was denied [by the Amorities to the Jews]. But, to fulfill his promises, God assisted the Israelites on this occasion since the land of the Amorites was to be given to them (*Questions on the Heptateuch* 4.44).

If offensive wars of this kind are justified in Augustine's eyes, it follows that defensive wars fall in the same category. Augustine comes close to saying as much when he argues (*City of God* 4.15) that a war can be considered

[49]Text: CSEL 28.3.3,353.

"felicitous" insofar as it prevents wrongdoers from ruling over the righteous, when he claims (*City of God* 19.7) that the "wrongdoing of the other side forces the wise man to wage just wars," and when he seems to concede that there was some justice in the claim that at times Rome's wars of expansion were justified: "One can exonerate Rome for undertaking and waging wars like this (i.e. which expanded her borders) because it was not the desire for human glory but the absolute need to protect its own liberty and safety that forced it to resist the violent attacks of its enemies" (*City of God* 3.10). Once again we have a clear contrast between an individual's rights in the matter of protecting life and property and a state's obligation in this area based on the absolute need to protect "its own liberty and safety."

The reasons for such distinctions are not hard to find if we recall Augustine's anxieties over the effects of human sin and his view of the state as a major bulwark against chaos and the dissolution of society. It would appear, indeed, that Augustine sympathizes with Cicero's view that although death is a natural event in the life of an individual, the same is not true of a state.

22.6[50]   In Book III of Cicero's *Republic*, unless I am mistaken, the point is made that a really good state never undertakes a war unless it is to live up to a treaty or to protect its safety. What the term 'safety' means here, or what kind of safety he has in mind, is made clear in another passage which reads 'When individuals are offered the chance for a quick death, they often manage to escape the kind of punishment that even the most insensitive of men experience, such as poverty, exile, imprisonment, and beating. But what appears to be a release from punishment in the case of individuals is for states a form of punishment itself because a state should be so constituted that it will go on

[50]Text: CCL 48.814.

forever. Death, then, is not at all a natural thing for states as it is for man. In his case it is not only inevitable but frequently desireable, but death for a state means that it is totally destroyed or snuffed out. On a miniature scale it is as if the entire world were to come to an end and collapse.' Cicero spoke this way because he agreed with the Platonists that the world will never end, and it is evident that what he had in mind was the state's undertaking war to maintain its perpetual existence in this world, as he himself says, even though individuals die and are born. All of this is like the olive tree with its perennial shade, or like the laurel and similar trees with their change of leaves. For individuals, then, death is not a punishment because it often frees them from retribution, but for the state it truly is a punishment (*City of God* 22.6).

Augustine goes on to discuss the tragic decision of the people of Saguntum in Spain who suffered annihilation at the hands of Hannibal in 219 B.C. because they chose to live up to their pact with Rome rather than to abandon that treaty for their own safety. Whatever his admiration for the Saguntines' courage, the bishop leaves the impression that their decision may not have been the wisest one. In any event, however uncertain Augustine may be on this philosophical point, he does not hesitate to praise those who have risked their lives in combat for the sake of bringing peace to the empire.

229.2[51] Those supremely brave and—what is more truly commendable—supremely loyal warriors who defeated a hitherto unconquered enemy and brought peace to the state and the provinces through their efforts and risks, aided as they were by the help of God's protection and succor, are glorious and deserving of praise (*Letter* 229.2).

[51]Text: CSEL 57.497.

Related to the issue of justifiable wars is the matter of civil wars and the right of individuals to engage in them. Given Augustine's preoccupation with the need for a "tranquility of order" and his views on the sufferings entailed in Rome's civil strife (*City of God* 3.27-30), it is not surprising that he has little sympathy for such conflicts. It is incumbent on men to resist temporal power when it commands something that is contrary to God's will (cf. *Letter* 185.2.8), but an individual's only recourse in such circumstances appears to be passive resistance. In this connection it should be remembered that Augustine had a highly paternalistic view of government, and that like many of his contemporaries he tended to view the citizenry not as "mature, rational persons who have a right to be consulted about their wishes," but as "willful passionate children who must remain permanently under the firm tutelage of a stern master" (Deane, 153). In such circumstances it is scarcely possible even to raise the issue of revolutionary wars.

The manner in which war should be conducted is not a topic which occupies much of Augustine's attention. On this score he adopts some of the contemporary traditions regarding the *ius in bello*, and he is influenced by the practice of the Old Testament. If, for example, God instructed Joshua to set up ambushes,

6.10[52]   This teaches us that such things are legitimate for those who are engaged in a just war. In these matters the only thing a righteous man has to worry about is that the just war is waged by someone who has the right to do so because not all men have that right. Once an individual has undertaken this kind of war, it does not matter at all, as far as justice is concerned, whether he wins victory in open combat or through ruses (*Questions on the Heptateuch* 6.10).

[52]Text: CSEL 28.3.428.

On the other hand, agreements made either with the enemy or with one's allies should be kept (*Letter* 189.6), and once peace had been achieved, mercy should be shown to the vanquished: "Just as we use force on a man as long as he resists and rebels, so, too, we should show him mercy once he has been vanquished or captured, especially when there is no fear of a future disturbance of the peace" (*Letter* 189.6). Although Augustine never addressed himself directly to the issue of non-combatants in war, his reaction to indiscriminate killing (*City of God* 1.4, 5 and 7) would indicate that he approved of the principle of non-combatant immunity.

An important dimension of the *ius in bello* is the subordinate's personal responsibility for carrying out the commands of his superior officer. In light of Augustine's feelings about the need for order and obedience at all levels of human society, it is not surprising that he leaves little room for questioning the legitimacy of a commander's orders. In his treatise *Against Faustus* (22.75), where he attempts to show that anyone fighting at God's command is acting in a responsible way, he uses the analogy of soldiers obeying their temporal sovereign.

22.75[53] Since, then, a righteous man, who happens to be serving under an ungodly sovereign, can rightfully protect the public peace by engaging in combat at the latter's command when he receives an order that is either not contrary to God's law or is a matter of doubt (in which case it may be that the sinful command involves the sovereign in guilt whereas the soldier's subordinate role makes him innocent), how much more innocent is involvement in war on the part of him who fights at the command of God, who, as everyone who serves him knows, cannot command anything evil. (22.75).

From this passage it is clear that in cases of doubt concerning the morality of a particular order the presumption

[53]Text: CSEL 25.673.

must be in favor of the commander, and the subordinate is obliged to obey. However, we must be wary of concluding from the statement, as several modern commentators have done, that "here, as in the case of the citizen's duty to obey the laws and the commands of the state, Augustine leaves no room for disobedience based upon the citizen's or soldier's individual decision that the command he receives is unjust or illegitimate" (Deane, 163). Augustine's statement applies only to situations in which the subordinate either has no problems or has only doubts about the legitimacy of the command. It says nothing about what must be done when the subordinate is *certain* that the order violates his conscience. In fact, Augustine seems never to have envisioned such a possibility in the sphere of military affairs. However, he did establish the principle that unjust laws are not to be obeyed (cf. *Letter* 185.2.8; *Discourse on Some Questions from Romans* 72), and he illustrates his point by citing the case of soldiers serving under the emperor Julian.

7[54]   Sometimes the authorities are good men who fear God; sometimes not. The Emperor Julian was an infidel, an apostate, a scoundrel, an idolater. Christian soldiers obeyed their emperor despite his lack of belief, but when it came to the issue of Christ, they acknowledged only Him who was in heaven. If Julian wanted them to honor idols or throw incense on the altar, they put God before him. But whenever he said 'Form a battle line' or 'Attack that nation,' they obeyed instantly. They distinguished between an eternal and a temporal master, but at the same time they were subject to their temporal master for the sake of their eternal one (*Commentary on Psalm 124*,7; cf. *Sermon* 62.8).

In the area of idolatry, of course, it was relatively easy for the common soldier to distinguish what was moral from

[54]Text: CCL 40.1841.

what was not and to determine where his responsibility lay. Nonetheless, the principle of discrimination itself is taken for granted by Augustine, and it is scarcely accurate to say that he viewed the common soldier as an automaton.

Since Augustine's views on religious coercion are related to the topic of violence, and since they went a long way in establishing Christian attitudes toward the suppression of heresy and the legitimacy of such things as crusades or holy wars, a very brief sketch of his thought on this matter is in order here. Any attempt to understand Augustine's outlook on this problem must needs underscore several assumptions which we have already seen operating in his thinking about war. Once again the devastating effects of sin and the danger posed for all men when sin goes unchecked loom very large in the bishop's mind. Once again the motive of fraternal correction and the desirability of winning over an opponent rather than of wreaking vengeance on him play an important role. Once again the polemical character of Augustine's thought comes to the fore. On this latter point we should remember that the bishop's ideas on coercion were developed during a long conflict with the Donatists, a conflict which was marked by a surfeit of charges and counter charges, with appeals to the secular arm by both sides and with no small amount of physical violence. In such a context it is hardly surprising that we find heated language and passionate argument. At the same time, however, when we speak of Augustine's endorsement of secular power to enforce orthodoxy, we should remember that he confines such coercive measure to fines, confiscation of property, exile and the like. For him, killing or maiming of dissidents is out of the question. If all these factors are kept in mind, it may at least be easier to see in its own context a religious attitude which is not only repugnant to modern thinking but often quite unintelligible.

The use of temporal power to insure religious conformity was a notion that Augustine came to accept only over a period of years. If it is an oversimplification to say that he simply changed his mind on the subject during the decades of controversy with the Donatists, it is at least apparent that his preoccupations changed as time progressed and that his developed ideas on the subject involve certain assumptions that were not very evident in the beginning. During the early years of his priesthood and episcopacy (i.e. ca. 392-400 A.D.) he makes clear that he has reservations about using coercion to bring heretics back into the Catholic Church. Writing to the Donatist bishop of Sinitum (near Hippo) in 392 A.D., he says,

23.7[55]   It is not my intention that anyone be forced into any community against his will but that the truth become clear to all who seek it in peace. From our side there will be no more threat of temporal powers, and let the same be true on your side with respect to the bands of Circumcellions [i.e. violent groups of Donatists]. Let us focus on the issue; let us argue rationally; let us depend on the authority of the Divine Scriptures. In peace and tranquillity let us, as far as possible, seek, and inquire, and knock, in order that we may receive, discover and have the door opened to us...(*Letter* 23.7).

And four years later he reiterates the point,

34.1[56]   God knows...that I do not want anybody forced into the Catholic community against his will. My only desire is that the truth be openly proclaimed to all men who are in error, and that once it has been made manifest through my ministry and God's assistance, it be persuasive enough to make them embrace and follow it (*Letter* 34.1).

At this early stage in his thinking Augustine is preoccupied with the need for uninhibited free choice in religious decisions and with the danger of bringing false converts (*ficti catholici*, as he calls them elsewhere [*Letter* 93.17])

55Text: CSEL 34.1.71.
56Text: CSEL 34.2.23.

into the Church by coercive methods. He did not favor such a tack, he remarks at a later date as he looks back at this period, because he was as yet unaware "to what lengths of evil they [the Donatist heretics] would dare go in their impunity or how much a sustained discipline (*diligentia disciplinae*) could contribute to changing them for the better" (*Reconsiderations* 2.31.2). Gradually, however, Augustine came to view the matter of religious dissent in another light, and by around 400 A.D. the issue of coercion began to take on new coloring. Freedom is now seen as part of a long process of admonishment and instruction, i.e. activities which perforce involve fear, constraint and external force. The problem of the *ficti* is left to the hidden workings of God's grace. What comes to the fore is the notion of punishment as a means of warning an individual or of inducing him to relinquish his position voluntarily. If coercion cannot of itself change a man's conduct or his internal disposition, it can at least make him reconsider his situation. Augustine makes this point more than once to his Donatist critics who argued that an appeal to secular forces not only violated an individual's freedom but ran counter to the spirit of the gospels.

2.84[57]   The difficulty or pain a man endures serves as an incentive to him to think about the reasons for his suffering. The purpose of it all is that if he discovers that he is suffering for justice's sake, he might embrace the good involved in undergoing such torments on behalf of justice. On the other hand, if he discovers that what motivates his suffering is actually evil and that his difficulties and trials are wasted, he might change his attitude for the better and, in one stroke, free himself both from useless torments and from the iniquity itself that will do him much more grievous harm. When rulers take action against you, then, you should regard it as an admonishment to think about why you are

[57]Text: CSEL 52.115.

receiving such treatment. If it is for justice's sake, then those rulers are indeed your persecutors, and you are the happy ones who will possess the kingdom of heaven because you have suffered persecution for justice's sake. But if you are suffering because of the iniquity of heresy, what are we to call those rulers but your admonishers. And what are you if not individuals who, just like any other criminals who pay the penalty of the law, will be unhappy both in this world and in the next. Nobody, then, is taking away your freedom, but you have to consider carefully what you really want. Do you want to be corrected and live in peace or do you want to persist in your wickedness and suffer punishment under the false claim of being martyrs (*Against the Letters of Petilianus* 2.84.186).

Far from seeing a conflict here with individual freedom, Augustine views the use of temporal power as a form of paternal correction and as a catalyst for effecting a change in an individual's outlook. His arguments on this score are not very different from those that he employed to justify both war and the coercive power of the magistrate, and once again he insists that the underlying motive is love.

2.94[58]   Howsoever we treat you we do so out of love for you...even when we are acting contrary to your own desires. Our aim is to have you change your outlook voluntarily and to live a reformed life. Everyone wants to avoid wrongdoing, but all the same a young boy is whipped against his will in order to learn this truth on his own, and the person doing the whipping is frequently the man who is dearest to him. And this is precisely what rulers would be telling you if they were in fact using

[58]Text: CSEL 52.139.

force on you because this is the purpose for which
their power has been ordained by God (*ibid.*
2.94.217)

In 408 Augustine explains to the Donatist bishop Vincentius that he altered his position on the use of coercion
because of the success that North African Catholic
bishops had had in reviving their communities through
such methods (*Letter* 93.5.16-17). Without the threat of
punishment, he contends, the heretics either because of
lethargy or an inability to break the bondage of custom
would never have been shocked into reexamining their
position and so would never have come to appreciate
their error. When coercion is applied, however, an individual "influenced by this fear rejects the error that he
was in the habit of defending or seeks the truth which he
knew nothing about and now voluntarily holds what he
earlier rejected" (*ibid.* 16). Elsewhere, in what must be
acknowledged as a partisan view, Augustine claims that
the Donatists themselves recognized the benefit they
received from the laws and punishments enacted against
heresy. ". . . Many have been reformed by means of those
laws and continue to be so every day. They give thanks
that they have been set straight and have been freed from
their destructive insanity" (*Letter* 185.2.7).

Although Augustine is at times very wary of putting
confidence in temporal rulers as a means of promoting
orthodoxy and strengthening the Church in its struggles
with heresy (see, for example, *Against the Letters of Petilianus* 2.97.224), he argues that Christian princes would
be acting irresponsibly if they did not use their power to
assure the Church's well-being, for "it is the responsibility
of Christian secular rulers to desire that their mother the
Church, whose spiritual offspring they are, enjoy peace
during their reign" (*Commentary on John's Gospel*
11.14). The emperor's role in this regard is succinctly
stated in the bishop's letter to Vincentius: "In truth let the
kings of the earth serve Christ even by legislating for him"
(*Letter* 93.5.19). That is precisely what was done, of

course, in the constitutions enacted by Theodosius and other emperors against dissenters, even, at times, to the point of prescribing the death penalty.

If it is claimed that there are no Scriptural foundations for this kind of appeal to secular authority, Augustine's answer is twofold. He acknowledges that no such appeal was made in the ages of the apostles and martyrs, but he contends that the contemporary situation is new, and that it calls for new policies. In fact, this use of secular power, Augustine argues, was prefigured in the Old Testament by the reign of Nebuchadnezzar, and what is currently taking place in the Catholic Church is a reflection of what occurred during the king's lifetime.

93.3[59]   In the time of the apostles and martyrs we find fulfilled what was prefigured when the king's practice was to force righteous and just individuals to worship his own image and sent them to a fiery death if they refused. Now, however, we find fulfilled what was prefigured subsequently by him after being converted to the worship of the true God. In this period he decreed that anyone in his kingdom who blasphemed against the God of Sidrac, Misac and Abdenago should be punished appropriately (*Letter* 93.3.9).

In sum, the principles of tolerance which were called for when the Church was a persecuted minority do not apply when she enjoys the favor of temporal powers. The problems involved in such a stance are not lost on Augustine, and, in his own mind at least, he justifies his position on the grounds of motive.

93.2[60]   It is clear both that wicked men have always persecuted the good and that good men have reciprocated. The former do harm by violating justice; the latter look out for others' interests by applying discipline. The former act in a savage way; the lat-

[59]Text: CSEL 34.2.453.
[60]Text: CSEL 34.2.452.

ter in a temperate one. The former are pandering to their own base desires; the latter are serving the interest of love.... Godless men have killed the prophets, and prophets have slain the godless; the Jews have scourged Christ, and Christ has scourged the Jews. Men turned the Apostles over to secular power; the Apostles handed men over to the power of Satan. In all these things the point to be noted is who is acting on behalf of truth and who on behalf of sin, who for purposes of doing harm and who for purposes of correcting others (*Letter* 93.2.8; cf. *Against the Leters of Petilianus* 2.19.43).

When specific New Testament examples of coercive action are demanded by the Donatists, Augustine cites the instance of St. Paul on whom Christ himself used physical force. "He not only restrained [him] with his voice but actually dashed him to the ground with his power. And to force him as he was raging in the darkness of disbelief to follow the light in his heart he first afflicted him with physical blindness" (*Letter* 185.22). Elsewhere (e.g. *Letter* 93.2.5) the bishop has recourse to the parable of the feast in *Luke* where the master who is dismayed over the lack of guests sends his servant to the highways and hedgerows with the injunction, "Compel them to come in." This short command (*coge intrare*) became almost a byword for Augustine's approach to heresy (cf. *Contra Gaudentium* 1.25.28; *Letter* 173.10; *Sermon* 112.7.8), and the justification for following such a tack is once again the fact that it is being done for the good of the recalcitrant and is motivated by love.

93.2[61]   In acting harshly against dissidents the Church, our true and lawful mother, is not repaying evil for evil. She is applying a beneficial discipline by driving out the evil of iniquity. She is not acting out of harmful feelings of hatred but a healing

[61]Text: CSEL 34.2.450.

spirit of love. When good and bad men do the same things, and when they suffer the same torments, it is not what they do or suffer that ought to distinguish them but the underlying reasons. Pharao oppressed the people of God with heavy burdens. Moses imposed harsh corrective measures on those same people when they acted in a godless way. The two men did the same thing, but they did not have the same beneficial purpose in mind. Pharao was puffed up with the lust for power; Moses was inflamed with love (*Letter* 93.2.6).

Augustine reiterates this theme in a homily on the *First Letter of John* where he confidently asserts that a man who truly loves cannot do harm: "Love and you cannot help doing good." And he explains:

10.7[62]   You may chastize but it is love that does this, not cruelty. You may strike but you do it for disciplinary reasons because your love for love itself does not permit you to leave the other person undisciplined. At times what comes from love and hatred seems self-contradictory. Hatred sometimes comes out in sweet tones and love in harsh ones (*Commentary on the First Letter of John* 10.7).

Both the inherent conflicts with freedom that are entailed in Augustine's approach to heresy and the grave abuses that can and did flow from that approach are easy to enumerate. But if love can mask a great many evils, and if there is some justification for viewing the Bishop of Hippo as the "prince of persecutors," it cannot be said that he was totally insensitive to the dangers that religious coercion posed. As we noted earlier, he did not endorse capital punishment or the maiming of dissidents, and, indeed, he claimed that the death penalty would actually discourage the practice of bringing heretics before the secular authorities at all (*Letter* 100.2). Moreover, such

[62]Text: SC 75.426.

extreme measures defeated the very purpose of the laws, which was not to inflict vindictive punishment but to make individuals reexamine their attitudes and actions. Even in the case of violent Donatists such as the Circumcellions Augustine does not want a literal interpretation of the *lex talionis* to apply, and in practice he did not hesitate (*Letter* 100.1-2; *Letter* 139.2) to appeal for leniency toward dissenters.

If Augustine's approach to religious coercion will scarcely withstand modern criticism, it is also true that the circumspection with which he viewed disciplinary action against heresy set him apart from many of his contemporaries and his followers in later ages. Without trying to justify his approach, one can say that he was more aware than they were that the perpetrators of coercion are as much affected by Adam's fall as their subjects are. If that fact is lost sight of the whole matter of religious conformity is quickly reduced to a simple case of the "righteous" overwhelming the "impious" for their "own good." If Augustine paved the way for such thinking, it is not true that he endorsed such an attitude.

5. *Pacifism in the Fourth Century*

Christian endorsement of war as a legitimate instrument of statecraft did not mean the complete disappearance of pacifist sentiments within the early Church. In addition to the prohibition against clerical participation in acts of violence, there were other signs that the difficulty of reconciling bloodshed and Christian love had not been surmounted. Much of the evidence on this score is couched in hagiographical and liturgical writings of the period, and one must be cautious about not making these sources bear more historical import than they can carry. At the same time, however, these documents provide insight into the popular thinking of the time, and it is interesting to observe how some of the arguments against militarism which were posed in the earlier period reappear after Christian participation in war is taken for granted. By and large these arguments will be uncomplicated by the issue of idolatry, and for that reason we will no longer have the problem of determining whether Christian opposition to war and military service is based on a refusal to kill or on the obligation to avoid worshipping an alien god.

This general principle, however, does not apply to the period of Julian the Apostate (361-363 A.D.) whose short rule of twenty months was marked by a persecution of Christians and a concerted effort to revive Rome's pagan heritage. During Julian's reign we have an account of two soldiers, Bonosus and Maximilianus, who were put to death when they refused to remove the Christian symbol (the labarum) from their military standards or to sacrifice to pagan deities when commanded to do so (*Acts of the Saints,* August 4.430-33). The same fate befell two members of the emperor's body guard, Juventinus and Maximinus, whom the sources (e.g. John Chrysostom, *Homily on the Holy Martyrs Juventinus and Maximinus,* 2-3; Theodoret, *History of the Church,* 3.15) tell us made disparaging remarks about the pagan revival under Julian and were arrested for treason. There is no suggestion in either of these instances that anti-militarism or opposition to killing entered into the picture. In fact, the assumption must be that there were no problems for these Christian soldiers at all until the element of idolatry was unexpectedly intruded where it had long since ceased to be an issue.

The same is not true, however, in the case of Martin of Tours, who is the most notable example of Christian opposition to war in the fourth century. According to his biographer, Sulpicius Severus, Martin had been forced into the army by his father at a very young age and had actually served for more than twenty years before he decided to give up his military career and devote himself unreservedly to the life of the spirit. Sulpicius gives us a very dramatic description of events surrounding this decision. The year is 356 A.D., and the scene is a place near

Worms in Gaul where Julian (subsequently the emperor) had already achieved a victory and was regrouping his forces for a final push into enemy territory. On the eve of an important battle Julian followed the not uncommon practice of distributing gifts to those troops under his command who had rendered meritorious service. Martin seized this occasion for redirecting his life, and in doing so he confronted in a personal way the problem of Christian faith and military service.

4.[63]   Meanwhile, when the barbarians were invading the provinces of Gaul, Julian Caesar, collecting his army at the city of the Vaugiones began the distribution of a donative to his troops. One by one the soldiers were called forward in the customary manner until it was Martin's turn. At that point, thinking that it was an appropriate time to be mustered out of the service—for he did not think it fair to accept the donative if he were not going to stay in the army—he said to Caesar, 'Up to the present I have served in your army; permit me now to be a soldier of Christ; it is not right for me to fight.'

On hearing this the tyrant went into a rage and said that Martin was withdrawing from the service not because of religious scruples but from fear of the battle that was about to take place the next day. Rather than being daunted by this kind of intimidation, Martin became even more determined, and he said, 'If my action is ascribed to craven fear rather than to faith, tomorrow I will take up a position at the front of the battleline without my arms. There, without shield or helmet but protected by the sign of the cross, I will in the name of the Lord Jesus break through the enemy's ranks without suffering injury. An order was given for him to be placed under guard so that he might

[63]Text: CSEL 1.114.

have the opportunity of living up to his proposal by being exposed to the barbarians without his armor. The next day the enemy sent a peace delegation and surrendered with all their property. Who would doubt that this victory was the work of the holy man and that it was given to prevent his being sent into the battle unarmed. Though the Holy Lord could have protected his soldier even in the midst of the enemy's swords and spears, he removed all necessity for fighting in order to prevent the saint's being offended by seeing other men die. For the only victory which Christ should offer on behalf of his soldier is one in which the enemy is defeated without anyone's being killed or wounded (*Life of St. Martin* 4).

The historicity of this account has been called into question by more than one scholar, and it can scarcely be denied that Sulpicius' description echoes certain ideas found in the *Acta* of military martyrs in the pre-Constantinian era, (e.g. Martin's claim that he was serving in the army of God and thus had no need for arms). What is significant, however, is that the biographer considers it one of Martin's glories that he could say "I am a soldier of Christ; it is not right for me to fight." Thus, at the end of the fourth century, when Sulpicus was writing, the adoption of an anti-militarist stance is presented as a commendable example for Christians to follow.

This point is understood by one of Martin's friends, Paulinus, Bishop of Nola (409-431 A.D.), who expresses his reservations about military life in a letter written to an unidentified acquaintance in the army. Paulinus exhorts the man to give up his career, and in very blunt terms he makes it clear that any service to Caesar which involves bloodshed is incompatible with the commands of Christ.

25.3[64]   Do not go on loving this world and the military service that is part of it because Scripture bears

[64]Text: CSEL 29.1, 225.

witness that anyone who is 'a friend of the world is an enemy of God' (*Letter of James* 4.4). The man who fights with the sword is an agent of death, and whoever sheds his own blood or someone else's will have death as his wages. He will be responsible for his own death or for the crime of bringing it on another because, of necessity, the soldier in war, even though he fights for someone else rather than himself, either meets death in defeat or attains victory through killing. One cannot be victorious except through shedding blood. For this reason the Lord says, 'You cannot serve two masters' (*Matt.* 6.24), that is, both the one God and mammon, both Christ and Caesar, although Caesar himself now wants to be the servant of Christ in order that he might deserve to be ruler over certain nations. For no earthly king is king of the whole world. That belongs to Christ who is God because 'all things were made through him, and without him nothing was made' (*John* 1.3). He is both the King of kings and the Lord of lords (*Rev.* 17.14). 'He does whatever he wishes on the earth, in the sea and in the depths (*Psalm* 135.6) (*Letter* 25.3).

We have an example of the kind of conversion that Paulinus is talking about here in the case of his friend Victricius, who was bishop of Rouen from about 380 to 407 A.D. Victricius had apparently been attracted to the religious life while he was serving in the army, and Paulinus gives us a vivid, albeit perhaps somewhat fictionalized, version of his friend's response to God's call. In a letter addressed to him Paulinus asks,

18.7[65] By what ways did (God) direct you to the path of His truth? Developing your spiritual strength through secular responsibilities he first made you a soldier before choosing you as his bishop. He let

[65]Text: CSEL 29.1.133.

you serve in Caesar's army in order to learn how to serve in God's. His design was to have you develop your strength for spiritual battles by hardening your body through the difficulties of camp life, fortifying your spirit for professing the faith at the same time that you strengthened your body for undergoing suffering. Later on, your departure from the service and your entrance into the spiritual life revealed what important plan Divine Providence had in mind for you. The moment you were inflamed with the love of Christ, the Lord Himself arranged an open display of what He had been doing. On a day set aside for the army to assemble, you entered the parade ground decked out in all the armor which you had already renounced in your inmost heart. Everyone took notice of your meticulous and fearful array when suddenly the whole army stood aghast as you turned, exchanged one oath for another and at the feet of the impious tribune you threw down your weapons of blood in order to put on the weapons of peace. Armed as you were with Christ, you disdained to be dressed in weapons of steel. When the old serpent's hatred inflamed the tribune with fury, you were scourged and beaten with sticks, but you remained unconquered because you depended on the wood of the Cross (*Letter* 18.7).

The letter goes on to describe how Victricius won his freedom with miraculous deeds and went on to pursue his new career. If the whole of the account is a conscious imitation of Martin's conversion, it is interesting once again to see themes from the earlier *Acta* reappearing (e.g. the comparison between the oath to Caesar and that to Christ, and the contrast between the arms of blood and the arms of peace). It should also be noted, however, that Victricius' military career is seen here as a kind of preparation for his ultimate calling and that the whole process is part of the divine plan. If, then, the military life is disparaged, it is not totally without redeeming values.

The same view is expressed in a hymn of St. Ambrose which was composed to honor the soldiers Victor, Nabor and Felix, who had been martyred in Milan in the era before Constantine. Although, as we have seen, Ambrose has a good deal to say about the legitimacy of bearing arms, he does not hesitate to extol the faith of the Church which tore these men "from the impious camps and consecrated them as soldiers of Christ" (*Hymn* 10.15-16). In their case, no less than in that of Victricius, their earlier careers had prepared them for their new life: "Their military efforts profited their faith. In being taught as soldiers to risk their lives for their ruler they were taught the seemliness of suffering for Christ" (17-20). No longer now do they have need for arms of steel because "the man who has the true faith is already clothed in armor" (23-24). The whole thrust of Ambrose's words revolves around the glory that accrues to those who abandon the force of arms for the *militia Christi*. It should be remembered that hymns of this kind were composed for liturgical purposes and thus were means of setting before the community models of Christian perfection. If Ambrose's words here do not gainsay his opinions on the legitimacy of war, they at least show another side to the issue, and they reflect an awareness that the Christian tradition regarding war and military service is a complex one.

Similar praise for soldiers who threw down their arms is found in Rome and Spain during these years in the last decade of the fourth century and the first decade of the fifth. An epigram of Pope Damasus honoring the memory of the military martyrs Achilles and Nereus says that after they had been engaged for some time in military duties, "They suddenly laid aside this madness, were converted and took to flight. They abandoned the impious camp of their leader. They threw down their shields and military trappings and bloody spears. Confessing Christ they rejoiced in carrying his triumphal sign" (*Epigram* 8.4-7). And in Calahorra, Spain the achievements of the military martyrs Emeterius and Chelidonius are commemorated in a hymn of Prudentius that was used in liturgical ceremonies in the cathedral of that city. Among the verses of that hymn (*Crowns of Martyrdom* I) we read the following:

34[66]   They abandon the banners of Caesar and choose the emblem of the cross. Instead of billowing serpent shapes on windblown flags they now carry before them the noble wood that crushed the serpent. Of little moment they deem it now to brandish spear at the ready, to strike the wall with war machine, to surround their camp with a ditch and to stain and defile their hands with bloody slaughter (*Crowns of Martyrdom I* 34).

And speaking in their own voices the two martyrs proclaim,

61   Let it be enough that we have spent our lives paying in full the bond we first gave to Caesar. Now is the time for giving to God what belongs to Him.

You captains of the banners, go. You tribunes take your leave. Remove the golden torques, the prize of bloody wounds. The glorious service of the angels now calls us away. Christ commands the white-robed cohorts there and reigning from his throne on high condemns to Hell those notorious deities and you yourselves who fashion silly monsters as your own special gods (*Ibid.* 61).

The arguments which prompt the martyrs' action here are scarcely new, and if we cannot prove from the words of this hymn that bloodshed was the primary reason for their abandoning the service, the context of Prudentius' lines would seem to support that position. What is important, however, is that praise is heaped on those who refuse to fight, and the hymn leaves little doubt that their action was meant to stir the faith and admiration of the community at Calahorra around the turn of the fourth century.

[66]Text: CCL 126.252; 253.

The foregoing is hardly meant to suggest that pacifist ideas either had a wide-spread appeal or remained a strong undercurrent in Roman society now that the Empire was on its way to becoming Christian. The dangers posed by barbarian invasions continued to mount, and, by and large, Romans, both Christian and pagan, endorsed the idea of fighting force with force. Indeed, by 416 A.D. this idea had become so entrenched that Theodosius II issued a decree stipulating that only Christians could serve in the army (*Theodosian Code* 16.10.21). What these texts do indicate, however, is that the endorsement of Christian participation in war was neither unopposed nor free of difficulties. The pacifist arguments of earlier centuries lived on, and if rejection of the *militia Caesaris* was by and large considered appropriate only for a limited few (i.e. the clergy), the tradition of non-violence was neither lost nor made an object of disdain.

Opposition to clerics' participation in warfare was trenchant and practically universal. On this score the feeling that bloodshed and Christian love were incompatible ran very deep, and clerics were expected to refrain from all forms of violence in order to minister to spiritual needs with an undivided heart. In fact, from the end of the fourth century there is evidence not only that a priest should not become a soldier but that former soldiers should not be candidates for the clergy. Thus Pope Siricius, writing to the Bishops of Africa in 386 A.D. (*Letter* 5.2) tells them of a decision by the Council at Rome which reads, "Anyone who has put on the military belt after his sins have been remitted must not be accepted into the clergy" (Canon 3). And less than a decade later Innocent I advised bishops meeting in Spain that, "No one who has served in the army following his baptism should be accepted into the clergy" (*Letter to the Synod at Toledo* 4). It is impossible to tell how widely or stringently these stipulations were adhered to, but they serve to underscore the longstanding practice in both pagan and Christian circles of separating priestly duties from military ones.

CONCLUSION

It is obvious from what we have seen that the developments which occurred in the fourth century regarding the legitimacy of war and military service brought no resolution to the problem of violence in a Christian context. Not only did pacifist sentiments retain some of their vigor, but the fact that military service continued to be forbidden to a certain segment of Christian society was an indication that it was not wholly consonant with Christian ideals. What is more, the limits established by the *ius belli* and the *ius in bello* were open to various interpretations, and their application was a difficult business under any circumstances. Thus, if there were tensions in the Christian community during the period before Constantine when total abstention from killing was the principle most trenchantly defended in our sources, these tensions remained after a new outlook developed.

It could not have been otherwise, for at the heart of the problem are two inescapable truths that are difficult to deal with in any society: the reality of sin and the necessity for preventing injury whenever possible. However pessimistic Augustine's assessment of the human condition may be, it is a healthy reminder of man's enormous capacity for doing evil and of the few resources at his disposal for restricting its effects on others. If Ambrose's principle about preventing injury is valid, it is valid in this context where even the ability to know clearly and unequivocally what response is called for is problematic. Thus, the absurdity of war and violence—however justified these may be by rational standards—is a product of the absurdity of sin and of man's obligation to do his best to limit its impact in a world that he neither fully understands nor fully controls.

The Christian's conception of his duty in this regard was different in the fourth century and later from what it had been in the first three. In the period before Constantine when he had little direct responsibility for managing affairs of state or maintaining internal and external order, his obligation was fulfilled more or less by obeying the law and living in harmony with his neighbor. In the fourth century, however, when he was immersed in contemporary social and political affairs and bore the responsibility for looking after the commonwealth, he was forced to wrestle with the ambiguities of power and the use of force. In this context he had to employ his wits to remain faithful both to his religious convictions and to the temporal demands which fell to his lot.

Inevitably the results of this effort were less than satisfactory. In seeking to limit the effects of sin man never escapes them himself, and it is hard to imagine any use of force that is not prone to excess. One could go further and acknowledge that there is some truth in the claim that the very notion of a Christian empire led to a kind of sanctification of the state and an alignment of ecclesiastical and temporal powers that undercut the Christian's capacity to work for peace. In this connection it has been suggested that Christians of the fourth century adopted the worse of two alternatives. Instead of endorsing war and military service they could have retained their mission as peacemakers and at the same time fulfilled their obligations to the state if they had chosen to confine their participation in violence to the kind of police action that was necessary to maintain a civil society. However, given the problems that Rome faced in securing its borders during the fourth and fifth centuries, it is difficult to see how Christians in positions of responsibility could have lived up to their obligations by following this tack. Moreover, at a more theoretical level, one must question whether the distinction between police duty and combat duty is more than an artificial one. By its very nature temporal authority involves the use of coercion, and once the legitimacy of coercion is acknowledged, the way is prepared for justifying war. It is this fact, I believe, which ultimately led to the changes that took place in Christian thinking during the fourth century. As one pacifist commentator has expressed it, "if the view that the government was an institution ordained by God implies the rightfulness, in some sense, of judicial penalties, it also implied the rightfulness, in some sense, of war. The fact that the police and the military were not distinguished, that the characteristic work of each was done with the 'sword', made it easy for ideas concerning the one to be transferred in the minds of Christians to the other" (Cadoux, *The Early Christian Attitude to War,* 204-5). In more generic terms one might say that if government is a legitimate agent for checking evil, it has much the same right to exercise its power against external threats as it does against internal ones.

Thus, a conditional acceptance of war and military service was in the offing from the very beginning. It may have been difficult for the Christian of the fourth century to reconcile this position with the peaceful import of the Gospels, but the need to do so was pressed upon him. If his answer was less clear-cut than that of his pacifist predecessor, it was more consonant with the problem he faced and with his own responsibilities in an imperfect world.

FOR FURTHER READING

Books and articles on war and military service in the early Church abound in every modern European language. I have limited myself in the following list to English sources (or foreign works translated into English) which proved most useful in preparing this volume. These works contain copious references to additional studies.

Aland, K., "The Relation between Church and State in Early Times: a Reinterpretation," *Journal of Theological Studies*, 19 (1968), 15-27. A good background article for understanding the nature of the problem of war and military service in the early Church.

Bainton, R.H., *Christian Attitudes Toward War and Peace. A Historical Survey and Critical Re-Evaluation* (Nashville 1960). A standard work albeit sometimes a bit simplistic in approach. A good place to begin one's study.

_____,"The Early Church and War," *Harvard Theological Review*, 39(1946), 189-212. A short but valuable study of important facets of the problem.

Brown, P.R.L., "The Attitude of St. Augustine to Religious Coercion," *Journal of Roman Studies*, 54(1964),107-16. A short but absolutely essential study for those interested in the problem of religious coercion.

Cadoux, C.J., *The Early Christian Attitude to War* (Oxford 1919). A good survey of the problem (with copious citations) from a pacifist point of view.

_____ , *The Early Church and The World. A History of the Christian Attitude to Paqan Society and the State down to the Time of Constantinus* (Edinburgh 1925). Broader in scope than the foregoing but useful for seeing the problem in a wider context.

Campenhausen, H. von, "Christians and Military Service in the Early Church" in *Tradition and Life in the Church,* trans. A.V. Littledale (Philadelphia 1968), 160-170. A short but perceptive (and balanced) essay on the whole issue.

Caspary, G.E., *Politics and Exegesis: Origen and the Two Swords* (Berkely 1979). Includes an excellent study of Origen's approach to war, especially in light of the Old Testament. See chapters I and IV.

Deane, H.A., *The Political and Social Ideas of St. Augustine* (New York 1963). A highly and justly praised study with generous citations. See especially chapters V and VI.

Eppstein, J., *The Catholic Tradition of the Law of Nations* (London 1935). An old treatise valuable mostly for its lengthy citations of early Christian writers.

Gero, S., "*Miles Gloriosus*: The Christian and Military Service According to Tertullian," *Church History*, 39 (1970) 285-98. A useful study of a very important figure in the history of the problem.

Harnack, A. von, *Militia Christi. The Christian Religion and the Military in the First Three Centuries*, trans. D.M. Gracie (Philadelphia, 1980). Originally published in German in 1905, this standard work is the starting point for almost all modern studies of the problem.

Hegeland, J., "Christians and the Roman Army: A.D. 173-337," *Church History*, 43 (1974), 149-163. A good survey of attitudes and practices in the early Church.

Hedgeland, John "Christians and the Roman Army from Marcus Aurelius to Constantine," *Aufstieg und Niedergang der Römischen Welt* 11.23.1 (New York 1979),724-834. A comprehensive study which focuses on Christian practices regarding war and military service but which includes an assssment of Christian writers (through the reign of Constantine) as well.

Hornus, Jean-Michel, *It is Not Lawful for me to Fight. Early Christian Attitudes towad War, Violence and the State*, rev. ed., trans. A Kreider and O. Coburn (Scottsdale, Pennsylvania 1980). The best recent study of the problem from a pacifist's point of view. Although a bit rambling in its organization, the work is a valuable contribution to the literature.

Marrink. A. ed., *War and the Christian Conscience: from Augustine to Martin Luther King, Jr.* (Chicago 1971). A collection of sources translated into English. Despite its title the work includes writers prior to Augustine, and it contains a very useful introduction.

Moffatt, J., in the *Dictionary of the Apostolic Church*, ed., J. Hastings, II (New York 1919), 646-73 *s.v.* "War." An old but handy reference which covers most of the sources and reflects the author's sound judgment.

Ryan, E.A., "The Rejection of Military Service by the Early Christians," *Theological Studies*, 13(1952), 1-32. A good survey from a non-pacifist point of view.

Russell, F.H., *The Just War in the Middle Ages*, (Cambridge 1975). An excellent study of the problem in the Middle Ages, this work contains a good chapter on St. Augustine.

Swift, L.J., "St. Ambrose on Violence and War," *Transactions and Proceedings of the American Philogical Association*, 101 (1970), 533-543.

Swift, Louis J., "War and the Christian Conscience I: the Early Years," *Aufstieg und Niedergang der Römischen Welt* 11.23.1 (New York 1979), 835-868.

Zampaglione, G., *The Idea of Peace in Antiquity*, trans. R. Dunn (Notre Dame 1973). Although the focus of the volume is peace, it contains much valuable information on our problem from both pagan and Christian points of view.